UNDERSTANDING

Isaac Bashevis Singer

Understanding Contemporary American Literature

Matthew J. Bruccoli, *Editor*

Understanding Bernard Malamud
by Jeffrey Helterman
Understanding James Dickey
by Ronald Baughman
Understanding John Hawkes
by Donald J. Greiner
Understanding Thomas Pynchon
by Robert D. Newman
Understanding Randall Jarrell
by J. A. Bryant, Jr.
Understanding Edward Albee
by Matthew C. Roudané
Understanding Contemporary American Drama
by William Herman
Understanding Vladimir Nabokov
by Stephen Jan Parker
Understanding Joyce Carol Oates
by Greg Johnson
Understanding Theodore Roethke
by Walter B. Kalaidjian
Understanding Mary Lee Settle
by George Garrett

UNDERSTANDING
Isaac
Bashevis
SINGER

By LAWRENCE S. FRIEDMAN

UNIVERSITY OF SOUTH CAROLINA PRESS

Copyright © University of South Carolina 1988

Published in Columbia, South Carolina, by the
University of South Carolina Press

Manufactured in the United States of America

Library of Congress Cataloging-in-Publication Data

Friedman, Lawrence S.
    Understanding Isaac Bashevis Singer / by Lawrence S. Friedman.
        p.   cm.—(Understanding contemporary American Literature)
    Biblicgraphy: p.
    Includes index.
    ISBN 0-87249-543-4. ISBN 0-87249-544-2 (pbk.)
    1. Singer, Isaac Bashevis, 1904–   —Criticism and interpretation.
2. Jews in literature. 3. Poland in literature. 4. New York (N.Y.)
in literature. I. Title. II. Series.
PJ5129.S49Z67   1988   87-33320
839'.0933—dc19   CIP

CONTENTS

EDITOR'S PREFACE

Understanding Contemporary American Literature has been planned as a series of guides or companions for students as well as good nonacademic readers. The editor and publisher perceive a need for these volumes because much of the influential contemporary literature makes special demands. Uninitiated readers encounter difficulty in approaching works that depart from the traditional forms and techniques of prose and poetry. Literature relies on conventions, but the conventions keep evolving; new writers form their own conventions—which in time may become familiar. Put simply, *UCAL* provides instruction in how to read certain contemporary writers—identifying and explicating their material, themes, use of language, point of view, structures, symbolism, and responses to experience.

The word *understanding* in the series title was deliberately chosen. Many willing readers lack an adequate understanding of how contemporary literature works; that is, what the author is attempting to express and the means by which it is conveyed. Although the criticism and analysis in the series have been aimed at a level of general accessibility, these introductory volumes are meant to be applied in conjunction with the works they cover. Thus they do not provide a substitute for the works and authors they introduce, but rather prepare the reader for more profitable literary experiences.

M. J. B.

UNDERSTANDING
Isaac Bashevis Singer

CHAPTER ONE

Understanding
Isaac Bashevis Singer

Career

Isaac Bashevis Singer was born in 1904 in Leoncin, Poland, into the long-vanished world of East European Jewry that his writing reinvokes. His youth was spent in a traditional household dominated by the ecstatic pietism of his father, the Hasidic (pietistic) rabbi Pinhos-Mendel Singer, yet tempered by the no less pious rationalism of his mother, Bathsheba, herself the daughter of generations of Bilgoray rabbis. The spiritual wealth and the material poverty of his upbringing fill the pages of *In My Father's Court* (1966), Singer's autobiographical account of his first eighteen years. Most of those years were spent on Krochmalna Street in Warsaw, the scene of his father's Beth Din, or rabbinical court. Into this "stronghold of Jewish Puritanism, where the body was looked upon as a mere appendage to the soul," the only valid education could be the religious instruction of the *heder* (religious primary school). To Pinhos-Mendel, whose "balcony was already a part of the street, of the crowd, of the Gentile world and its savagery," secular learning was the badge of worldliness. And the world itself was *tref* (unclean). "Many years were to pass," writes Singer, "before I began to understand how much sense there was in this attitude."[1]

The lure of the world beneath his father's balcony was soon personified in his older brother, Israel Joshua, who in 1914 at the age of twenty-one moved into an artist's studio. There the ten-year-old Isaac first met the intelligentsia who had discarded their traditional beliefs with their Jewish gaberdines. Impassioned conversations were carried on in Polish as well as in Yiddish by "emancipated" Jews who neither prayed nor observed the dietary laws. Girls casually smoked cigarettes and shamelessly posed nude. "This was quite a change from my father's studio, but it seems to me that this pattern has become inherent to me. Even in my stories it is just one step from the study house to sexuality and back again" (240).

It was also in 1914 that Singer read his first secular book—*Crime and Punishment* in Yiddish, a gift from Israel Joshua. The blend of loneliness, irrationality, and criminality of Dostoevski's

Raskolnikov would profoundly influence Singer's writing. In his 1967 preface to a new edition of Knut Hamsun's *Hunger,* Singer noted the "strong resemblance" between Raskolnikov and Hamsun's hero, while acknowledging the debt his fiction owed to Dostoevski and Hamsun. Only the influence of Israel Joshua himself would prove more decisive.

In 1917 Singer accompanied his mother to Bilgoray, her remote native village, which had remained "pretty much the same as it must have been during the time of Chmielnicki. . . . I could have written *The Family Moskat* without having lived in Bilgoray, but I could never have written *Satan in Goray* or some of my other stories without having been there."[2] Far from the worldliness of Warsaw, Singer would spend four formative years in that quintessential setting for so much of Yiddish literature—the primitive East European Jewish village called the *shtetl.* Later he would draw upon Bilgoray's abundant imaginative resources not only for the seventeenth-century locales of *Satan in Goray* and *The Slave,* but for an entire network of moral, psychological, and social attitudes: "In this world of old Jewishness I found a spiritual treasure trove. I had a chance to see our past as it really was. Time seemed to flow backwards. I lived Jewish history" (290). Yet it was also in Bilgoray that

Singer sought out the "enlightened" watchmaker Todros, whose conversation and library of secular books he would re-create in Jekuthiel, the watchmaker who initiates Asa Heshel into the modern world in *The Family Moskat*. And when post–World War I American aid to Polish villages provided Yiddish translations of European authors along with sacks of white flour, young Singer first read Strindberg, Turgenev, Tolstoi, Maupassant, and Chekhov. But it was the philosophy of Spinoza that "created a turmoil in my brain. His concept that God is a substance with infinite attributes, that divinity itself must be true to its laws, that there is no free will, no absolute morality and purpose—fascinated and bewildered me" (305). An equally fascinated and bewildered Asa Heshel endlessly pores over his volume of Spinoza in *The Family Moskat*. More than any other author, Spinoza shook Singer's Jewish orthodoxy.

In 1921 Singer agreed to enroll in the Tachkemoni Rabbinical Seminary in Warsaw, the price of his refusal to accompany his mother and younger brother Moishe to another *shtetl* where his father was to take up a rabbinical post. Bored by his studies and nearly starving in Warsaw, Singer fled to Bilgoray, where he eked out a bare living as a Hebrew teacher. By 1923 he was back in Warsaw working as a translator and as a proofreader for *Literarische Bletter,* a Yiddish literary magazine which published his first stories. It was during the 1920s that Singer forged the language, the style, and the subject matter of his mature fiction. Israel Joshua had suffered through a period of disenchantment with the Yiddish language as a literary medium and with Jewish materials as subject matter, which had led him to creative impotence. Finally resolving his dilemma by returning to Yiddish and Jewishness, he wrote *Yoshe Kalb* (1932), the book which won him an international reputation and propelled him to America. In a 1966 introduction to *Yoshe Kalb* Singer cites his brother's spiritual and physical revival as an example of "what the right theme can do for a writer." Perhaps Israel Joshua's struggles confirmed the younger Singer's decision to follow his own inclinations and to eschew the demands for contemporary "relevance" then fashionable in Warsaw literary circles. The result was Singer's first novel, *Satan in Goray,* begun in 1933, serialized in 1934, and published in book form in 1935. Set in seventeenth-century Poland, this demon-ridden tale of Messianic fanaticism established the exotic idiom of much of his later work. (Like *Satan in Goray,* all of Singer's subsequent novels are first written and serialized in Yiddish, even those which initially appear in book form in English translation.)

By the early 1930s little remained for Singer in Warsaw. His mistress, Runya, a fervent Communist, was preparing to take their son Israel to Russia. Singer's father had died in 1929, the year of his son's birth; his mother and younger brother remained in Galicia; and his married sister was in England. So in 1935 Singer followed Israel Joshua to New York, becoming a free-lance writer for *Der Forverts (The Forward)*, the Yiddish daily with which he remains associated. He had left behind not only family and friends but the wellsprings of his imagination and the vital Yiddish culture of Warsaw:

When I came to this country I lived through a terrible disappointment. I felt then—more than I believe now—that Yiddish had no future in this country. In Poland, Yiddish was very much alive when I left. When I came here it seemed to me that Yiddish was finished: it was very depressing. The result was that for five or six or maybe seven years I couldn't write a word. Not only didn't I publish anything in those years, but writing became so difficult a chore that my grammar was affected. I couldn't write a single worthwhile sentence.[3]

The creative impasse was broken in 1943 with the

reissue of *Satan in Goray* along with five new short stories. Like *Satan in Goray,* the stories, among them the brilliant "Destruction of Kreshev" and "Zeidlus the First," are tales of demonic possession.

Events of the next decade would determine the direction and reception of Singer's fiction. Israel Joshua's death in 1944 led Singer to begin *The Family Moskat* in the following year. This long family chronicle, the sort of book his older brother had written, may have represented an attempt to continue the work, or to emerge from the long shadow, of the revered Israel Joshua. Singer dedicated *The Family Moskat* "to my late brother, I. J. Singer, author of *The Brothers Ashkenazi.* To me he was not only the older brother, but a spiritual father and master as well." Serialized in *The Forward* from 1945 to 1948 and published in book form in Yiddish and in English in 1950, *The Family Moskat* was Singer's first novel to appear in English, selling 35,000 copies in translation. It established not only Singer's command of a realistic genre far removed from the spirit-haunted world of his earlier work, but his potential non-Yiddish audience as well.

When Saul Bellow published his own translation of Singer's masterful story "Gimpel the Fool," in the May 1953 issue of *Partisan Review,* he won for its author the sort of modernist cachet and mainstream acceptance that no Yiddish writer had hitherto enjoyed. Since then, nearly all of Singer's prolific output, whether in the fantastic mode of *Satan in Goray* or in the realistic mode of *The Family Moskat*, has reached an increasingly large and respectful audience. Having lived longer in America than in Poland, he has nevertheless retained his essential subject matter: "I deal," wrote Singer in his preface to *Passions* (1975), "with unique characters in unique circumstances, a group of people who are still a riddle to the world and often to themselves—the Jews of Eastern Europe, specifically the Yiddish-speaking Jews who perished in Poland and those who emigrated to the U.S.A." In his eighteen volumes of fiction, comprised equally of novels and short stories; in his memoirs; and even in his many tales for children, Singer has all but single-handedly kept alive a vanished past and a dying language. His many literary honors, culminating in the 1978 Nobel Prize, testify to the power of his lonely dedication.

Overview

Moral struggle dominates Singer's fiction. As in medieval morality plays where good and evil angels wage war on the battlefield of man's soul, Singer's works pose the eternal moral question: How is one to live? To answer this question Singer's characters are forced to choose between two worlds. And upon their answer much depends, for heaven and hell, ubiquitous in Singer's fiction, await the choice. The physical environment serves mainly as a locus for antithetical states of mind or being. Settings and characters alike reflect Singer's dualistic world view, and are often paired to dramatize moral alternatives. Thus Miriam Lieba's choice of the sensual Gentile Lucian over the pious Jew Jochanen destroys her life in *The Manor*, while her father, Calman Jacoby, is redeemed in the same novel by abandoning his estate for the study house.

Singer's characters invariably grow up in a traditional Jewish home which in itself embodies a moral decision. Imbued with the letter and the spirit of Jewish law as contained in the Torah (five books of Moses) and the Talmud (the body of written Jewish law), the home is the repository of those moral values expressed by "Jewishness." As such, it represents a state of mind, a way of life, an ultimate spiritual destination. Whether by choice or by necessity Singer's protagonist learns that the path of righteousness leads homeward. Wisdom lies not in the apprehension of things unknown but in the regaining of things lost or forgotten. Singer's fiction is therefore filled with penitents who, seduced temporarily by worldly lures and aspirations, return to the faith of their fathers. Penitence involves a deliberate contraction, an ironic foreclosure of possibilities: Yasha Mazur (*The Magician of Lublin*) walls himself into a study house; Joseph Shapiro (*The Penitent*) reverts to Orthodox earlocks and gaberdines in Israel.

Orthodox Judaism is an intensely patriarchal religion, centered upon God the Father. Its stress on the primacy of male worship extends even to the separation of men and women in the synagogue. Pious men like Singer's father are forbidden to look directly at women, and "it did not behoove a Hasidic young man to walk in the street with a girl—even his sister" ("Guests on a Winter Night"). Hasidim routinely abandon their wives and children to spend long holidays at the courts of wonder (miracle-working) rabbis. Obeying the Hasidic injunction to worship God not in sorrow but in joy, they pray, feast, sing, and dance, forging male bonds as strong as their links to family. A life of scriptural study is man's highest calling, and wealthy Jewish families willingly support scholarly sons-in-law during the first several years of marriage if not longer. Learning is so prized that humble workers are inordinately proud if their smattering of Hebrew unlocks the meaning of the holy texts. Combined with Hasidic wanderlust, the ideal of ceaseless study constitutes a mode of evasion, a strategy for withdrawing from the world. In an unclean world the pallor of the study house becomes a badge of piety. Poverty is another. A recurring figure in Singer's fiction is the unkempt rabbi poring eternally over the Talmud in his unheated study, oblivious to cold and hunger. Revered by Jews, such holy scholars are among Singer's most sympathetic characters.

While the men pray and study, the work of the everyday world is carried on by women. Singer recalls the daughter who assists her goose-dealer mother while her husband, "a delicate young man, spent his time being Jewish, and often visited Radzymin for months" (157). A man may pay such visits to his rabbi's court, but a woman functions primarily as wife and mother: spinsterhood and barrenness are abhorred by a society in which a girl's eagerness to marry is matched only by her eagerness to reproduce. If man's highest calling is to study Jewish texts, woman's is to bear Jewish children. Childless women resort first to prayers, then to amulets and exorcists in attempting to conceive. Particularly desperate is the eponymous heroine of "Altele," "forever making journeys to holy men, miracle workers, and even witches, fortune tellers, and sorcerers." Overt sexuality is anathema, and feminine beauty, while appreciated, is frequently equated with worldly temptation. To a Hasid forbidden to glance even at female relatives, women are eternal Eves luring men to their destruction. Silent and submissive women are valued most highly: the old rabbi's wife who rouses herself in the middle of the night to fan the coals under the samovar of her studying husband ("The Shadow of a Crib"); Tsipele, Calman Jacoby's youngest daughter, who unquestioningly accepts the husband chosen by her father (*The Manor*). Deviants from the feminine ideal end badly: Zirel, beautiful and well educated but "full of desire," is dragged off to hell by an imp who plays upon her vanity and boredom ("The Mirror"); even Yentl, driven by love of Torah to disguise herself as a young man in order to study at the yeshiva, meets with only fleeting success ("Yentl the Yeshiva Boy").

Singer clings tenaciously to the moral value of Jewish stereotypes even in his later fiction. As a modern man who goes so far as to question the virtue of having children in the post-Holocaust world, Singer knows that traditional Jewish values survive mostly in memory. Divorced from their Hasidic context the ideals of masculine piety and feminine meekness seem quixotic in contemporary

New York—or in Israel, for that matter. Since few saints inhabit Singer's later fiction, virtue comes to consist chiefly of a kind of negative capability. Shaken or deficient in faith, the virtuous can at least refuse to be party to the grosser abominations. Yet the ancient stereotypes persist as standards by which modern men and women are implicitly measured, and by which they can regain their lost identity as Jews. Joseph Shapiro (*The Penitent*), perhaps Singer's most misanthropic hero, wrenches himself free from the spiritual wasteland of New York. Fleeing to Israel, he dons Hasidic garb, marries the silent and pious Sarah, and, by a conscious leap of faith, relives the Jewish past.

Such characters as Shapiro and Yasha Mazur accept enclosure as the necessary antidote to an unclean world. And for Singer the concept of *tref* (unclean) extends far beyond the Gentile world of lust and violence depicted in *The Slave* to an all-embracing vision of the world as a whole. It is the natural product of Jewish life in both of Singer's characteristic settings—the *shtetl* and Warsaw. The *shtetl* Jew, existing on the fringes of a backward agricultural economy and generally barred from owning land, was no better off than the city Jew, crowded into a fetid ghetto and often barred from universities and professions. *Shtetl* and city Jew alike were periodically subjected to indignities and worse by their Gentile rulers, whether Poles, Russians, or Germans. The history of Polish Jewry from the pogrom unleashed by Chmielnicki in 1648 (*Satan in Goray*) to the onslaught of Hitler's Nazis in 1939 (*The Family Moskat*) is written in the blood of innocents. Aside from *Satan in Goray* and scattered stories, nearly all of Singer's works are composed after the Holocaust gave his recurring negation of the world its most powerful historical rationale. Little wonder that Singer's Jews fear and abhor the world beyond the Jewish pale.

Surrounded by an unclean world, Singer's characters must decide how best to live in it. Their decisions invariably propel them toward one of the polar opposites of the Jewish experience: Hasidism or Haskalah. Hasidism (pietism), a revivalist movement of religious enthusiasm and ecstasy, was born in eighteenth-century Poland. Its founder, the Baal Shem Tov, was a legendary *zadik* (wise man) whose powers apparently extended to the miraculous healing of the sick and the lame. Disciples imbued with the Hasidic concept of a life devoted to religious rapture proselytized so effectively that soon nearly every Jewish community in Poland had a court presided over by a *zadik*. Singer's fiction is crowded with Hasidim who argue the virtues of their wonder-working rabbis, to whose courts they flock on Jewish holidays, there to serve God in the joy of song and dance. Such a Hasid is Reb Moshe Ber ("The Old Man"). Ragged, starving, bereft of family, and beset by visions of the Angel of Death, he trudges across Poland from Warsaw to Galicia, driven by his desire to celebrate the holidays with his fellow Turisk Hasidim in Jozefow. Venerated because he once sat at the table of a famous wonder rabbi, Reb Moshe Ber is given a house and a forty-year-old bride by the Turisk Hasidim. Nine months later she gives birth to a son who will one day say the essential Kaddish (prayer for the dead) over his father's grave. "The Old Man" is a parable of Jewish survival. By invoking the Hasidic court as the site of Reb Moshe Ber's salvation, the story provides a powerful solution to the dilemma of Jewish existence. Again and again Singer returns to the Hasidic court along with the family to symbolize Jewish communal life, apart from which his individual Jews find existence either perilous or meaningless.

Yet the mystic joys of Hasidism were not for everyone. The Haskalah (enlightenment), originating in mid-eighteenth-century Germany and generated by merchants and intellectuals, represented an attempt to cope with secular modernism by reconciling it with traditional Judaism. By translating the Pentateuch into German, Moses Mendelssohn, the outstanding Haskalah scholar, not only made the Bible more accessible to his fellow Jews but implicitly endorsed German as the language of everyday life. A businessman as well as a philosopher, yet an observant Jew in private life, Mendelssohn shaped his career to demonstrate that a Jew could win approval and recognition from the Gentile world without surrendering his essential Jewishness. The clash between this Haskalah desire to face the modern world and the Hasidic reflex to flee from it plays an important part in Singer's fiction and family recollections alike. His brother Israel Joshua, viewed by their father as "wallowing in heretic literature, painting indecent pictures," is Singer's first enlightened Jew: "Although opposed to piety, he was aware of the faults of worldly existence. . . . Inclined toward socialism, he was at the same time too skeptical to have that much faith in humanity. My father summed up my brother's point of view with, 'Neither this world nor the world to come . . . ' " (232). Asa Heshel (*The Family Moskat*) and Ezriel Babad (*The Manor*) are but two of the most important among Singer's many Jews caught between two worlds and comfortable in neither.

By 1900 many thoughtful Jews had concluded that neither Hasidism nor the Haskalah provided completely satisfactory models for living. While the former seemed increasingly anachronistic, the latter produced scant rewards. Whether rejected or embraced, Gentiles persisted in regarding Jews as aliens among them. Those Jews who found both piety and assimilation impossible gravitated toward either of two new movements: Zionism and socialism. Each had millenial goals: returning to the Palestinian homeland, for Zionists; altering European society, for socialists. And each had affinities with the two older Jewish movements. Like Hasidim, Zionists rejected the world around them; like the enlightened, socialists put their trust in that world, albeit a world they hoped to transform. Especially in his long novels dealing with Jewish life from the late nineteenth century until the rise of Hitler, Singer inserts debates among proponents of the various Jewish movements. Thus Mirale, Ezriel Babad's sister, preaches socialism via violent revolution; Aaron Lipman, her more squeamish socialist friend, finally breaks with the movement, arguing that the only viable life for Jews must be sought in Palestine (*The Manor*). While the socialist dream of remaking the known world seemed at first more attractive—and attainable—to Jews than the Zionist dream of a Jewish homeland in a world unknown, it was to prove the less powerful vision. Singer's Jewish socialists are Jews first, comrades only incidentally, to their Gentile cohorts. Asa Heshel lives the Communist dream as nightmare during a forced sojourn in the Soviet Union. At the end of *The Family Moskat* he opts to remain in Nazi-besieged Warsaw rather than flee eastward to "freedom." Either choice is hopeless.

Equally "enlightened" and far more competent and mature than Asa Heshel, Ezriel Babad decides to flee "hate-ridden" Europe for Palestine at the end of *The Estate.* Yet his decision, as presented by Singer, is taken less in joy than in weariness and sorrow. Undeniably preferable to assimilation or socialism (itself merely a failed version of assimilation), emigration, whether to Palestine or to America, risks the loss of Jewish identity. In much of Singer's later fiction New York is seen as a modern Gehenna (hell), and Paris, London, and even Tel Aviv are little better. More and more the modern world comes to resemble the unclean Warsaw beneath his father's balcony. And his fictional alter egos are presented as restless, dissatisfied, alienated. The term "enlightened" comes to identify—exclusively and ironically—those Jews who have lost their path in trying to find it.

For Singer the "world is finally but lure and appearance, a locale between heaven and hell, the shadow of larger possibilities."[4] The heroic conquest of the material world, so dear to Western literature, is rendered meaningless in his fiction. Singer's is rather an antiheroic ideal represented by two recurring figures drawn from traditional Yiddish literature: the *baal-teshuvah* (penitent) and *dos kleine menshele* (the common man). "Repentance, a central concept in Judaism, applies to the believer who sins and to the unbeliever who returns. Sometimes it seems that the tradition extends a greater measure of divine grace to the *baal-teshuvah*. The Midrash [rabbinic commentary] says that God goes halfway to meet those who return."[5] Rabbi Bainish of Komarov ("Joy"), who has buried his children, despairs of God's mercy and finally of God himself. Sick at heart, he is first cheered by a vision of Rebecca, his lost youngest daughter. On his deathbed he sees another vision—of his dead sons and daughters, father and grandfather, between the doorjambs, arms outstretched. His final words, "One should always by joyous," reaffirm his faith in God's dispensation. No overt act of penance is required of a Rabbi Bainish whose momentary doubt is the only blemish on an otherwise holy life. But from those who forgot their Jewishness or abandoned it for the vanities of worldly success, more is demanded. Characters such as Yasha Mazur (*The Magician of Lublin*) and Joseph Shapiro (*The Penitent*) must first renounce the world, then refashion their Jewish identity.

The *baal-teshuvah* is invariably a thinker whose

change of heart and way of life results from agonizing reappraisal. *Dos kleine menshele,* by contrast, leads a relatively unexamined, instinctive life rooted in family and community. His prototype in Yiddish literature is Sholem Aleichem's Tevye the Dairyman. Abba Shuster, the paterfamilias of Singer's poignant "The Little Shoemakers," embodies a tradition of dedicated craftsmanship extending from the seventeenth to the twentieth century, from the Frampol *shtetl* to the New Jersey suburbs. Gathered around the cobbler's bench with his seven sons and singing an old Frampol song once again in America, Abba thankfully concludes: "They had not forgotten their heritage, nor had they lost themselves among the unworthy." The story's ending is a paean to the survival of the individual through the reestablished Jewish family. Another version of *dos kleine menshele* appears in Singer's stories of holy innocents more fit for heaven than for earth. Such a saint is Aunt Itte Fruma ("Guests on a Winter Night"), who loses her house and gives away her few possessions, since "One takes nothing to heaven except good deeds." Shortly after her death Singer's father pronounces her epitaph: "She gave up a house in Frampol and built herself a mansion in Paradise." Still another variant of *dos kleine menshele* is found in Singer's most famous story, "Gimpel the Fool."

Gimpel is a *schlemiel*, one of those gullible and powerless, yet oddly wise, fools that inhabit much of Yiddish fiction. A throwback to I. L. Peretz's Bontsha, whose humility shames even the heavenly angels, Gimpel is pious and uncomplaining, a willing dupe whose reward, like Bontsha's and Itte Fruma's, will be paradise.

Little of Singer's fiction invokes the earthly paradise awaiting Abba with his sons in New Jersey. Far more often the hope of heaven alone makes life on earth bearable. Because this is so, the problem of belief is central to Singer's work. Belief in God was a natural by-product of *shtetl* life. All but totally ignorant of a world beyond their family and community, Jews could hardly have broken the circle of traditional belief even had they so wished. With the breakup of the *shtetl* world came the sort of mini-diaspora (scattering of the Jews) evident in Singer's own family history. Jews who moved to Warsaw faced challenges to their beliefs undreamed of in Bilgoray. And when many of these same Jews emigrated, most often to America, their consequent loss of Jewish identity shook their belief still further. With the dissolution of social bonds comes the chaos that Singer eventually equates with the loss of belief. In "Stories from Behind the Stove," Meir the eunuch, one of Singer's holy madmen, claims that only God's word holds the world together: "If he takes His word back, the whole creation returns to primeval chaos." Since the world exists only by God's sufferance, to deny Him is to invite the very chaos He mercifully wards off. Unfortunately this simple belief was undermined by the cataclysmic fact of the Holocaust.

While questions about God's plan for His chosen people are endemic to Jewish thought, they take on a macabre irony after the Holocaust. At the very least, the Holocaust seemed to beg the question of God's nature. How could any but a malevolent God sanction the slaughter of innocents? And how is it possible that God, the principle of order, could unleash the ultimate chaos? In "The Son," Singer itches to ask a Lithuanian rabbi why the Torah hadn't prevented the death of Jewish millions in Hitler's crematoriums. But he already knows the answer: "To be martyred in God's name is the highest privilege." Only God, the "Almighty Knower," has all the information; humans must make do with "crumbs of facts." If not proof of God's inscrutability, the Holocaust may be evidence of His wrath. Singer's alter ego in "The Mentor" recalls Isaiah's admonition of doom: "A sinful nation, a people laden with iniquity, a seed of evildoers. . . . They have forsaken the Lord. They have provoked the Holy One of Israel." To regard the Holocaust dead either as martyrs or as victims of God's wrath is equally farfetched. Singer's point is that not even the Holocaust can release his people from the burden of belief.

After Hitler belief is more crucial than ever. Without God, "There is no reason one should not be a Nazi" ("The Mentor"). The ashes of the dead who were burned and the remains of their Nazi murderers would share precisely the same fate if the spirit did not exist. If the decay of the body is the end of human existence, then the impossibility of ultimate justice renders life meaningless. While Singer cannot deny the madness around him, he refuses to accept its finality. Instead he transmutes it into a single aspect of a dualistic world view that opposes chaos to order, flesh to spirit. Violence arises in Singer's fiction from an implicit denial of the human spirit. Victims become mere hunks of flesh for murderers from Chmielnicki to Hitler. And one transgression begets another: Risha's blood lust leads to carnal lust for Reuben the butcher, whose slaughtering of animals she at first avidly watches, and then joins ("Blood"). Bloodshed leads Risha to adultery and deception, then to Christian conversion, and finally to transformation into a werewolf. Lost belief (communion) and even lost humanity (transformation) are the tragic consequences of blood lust. Horror at the taking of animal life, which can so easily lead to the taking of human life, drives many Singer characters to the vegetarianism espoused by the author himself.

Risha's descent into darkness hints at the enveloping chaos of the Holocaust. Not to believe in God is to accept one or another version of chaos as a permanent condition. To the extent that the Holocaust forced a redefinition of human nature, order in an older sense may no longer be possible. In "The Cafeteria," Singer sees degeneration everywhere. The disintegrating human brain adumbrates the crumbling of civilizations: New York "has all the symptoms of a mind gone berserk." Yet Singer goes on writing, lecturing, paying taxes: To behave as if one will go on living is to reaffirm the principle of order. Since that principle resides in God, belief is a condition of life itself. Old Boris Merkin, "without legs, without friends, without a family," has survived Stalin's Siberian death camps ("The Cafeteria"). Sitting in his wheelchair in New York he reads newspapers and "still hopes for a just revolution." For his daughter, herself a survivor of Russian and German prison camps, everything ends in death, and hope is futile. "Hope in itself is a proof that there is no death," replies Aaron/Singer.

Opposed to such positive figures as the saint, the penitent, the wise fool, and the hopeful skeptic are a host of characters whose faith is misplaced or nonexistent. Adele's madness for clothes ("The Primper") leads her to reject suitors with open collars or unbuttoned coats, to squander her inheritance on the latest Paris fashions, and to gossip about dresses and jewelry in the synagogue instead of praying. In her old age, still babbling about her outfits, she converts to Christianity, "because she wanted to be bedecked in her grave": Christians are dressed in all their finery for the coffin, but luxurious burial clothes are forbidden to Jews. Although Adele's is a comically trivial obsession, it leads nonetheless to estrangement from her people and from her God. Zeidel Cohen's passion—for books—takes a higher form but is no less destructive ("Zeidlus the Pope"). A Jewish Dr. Faustus, Zeidel, in his intellectual pride, lays himself open to Satan's flattery. Convinced by Satan that the Jews hate greatness and that the Christians will idolize him and one day crown him Pope Zeidlus the First, he converts. Years later, blind and destitute, his pride shattered, Zeidel is dragged off by Satan to hell. Like so many of Singer's Promethean strivers, Zeidel has lost both this world and the next. A still more harrowing story of obsession and loss is told in "The Gentleman from Cracow." An entire village is consumed by fire in one of Singer's most apocalyptic visions of the wages of sin: "but it was the infants who had been the real victims of the passion for gold that had caused the inhabitants of Frampol to transgress. The infants' cribs were burned, their little bones were charred. The mothers stooped to pick up little hands, feet, skulls." Employing the imagery of the Holocaust, Singer evokes the ultimate tragedy of lost or misplaced faith.

In Singer's dualistic world where people must choose between the eternally warring forces of good and evil, free will is essential. Less concerned with the collective Jewish experience that is the product of uncontrollable historical forces than with individual fate, Singer portrays a world of moral antitheses. God created Satan so that man might freely choose between them; without evil, choice is rendered meaningless and the moral dilemma evaporates. And evil has its attractions and its ostensible rewards, or nobody would choose it. To represent various states of evil Singer relies heavily upon the grotesque. His many imps and demons—attractively disguised and smooth-talking—lie in wait to trap his Everyman who eddies between antithetical pairs: heaven and hell; reason and passion; order and chaos. Demonology provides a kind of shorthand for human motivation. A character's spreading moral stain is often explained by the powerful workings of his per-

sonal demon. Sometimes these demons act as narrators. "From the Diary of One Not Born" is told
by an imp whose nasty tricks, running the gamut
from stinging a rabbi's nose to driving an innocent
village woman to suicide, earn the commendation
of Asmodeus (Satan) himself. And the same Asmodeus condemns the demon narrator of "The
Last Demon" to an eternity in backwater Tishevitz
for failing to corrupt the village's rabbi. While
hardly a profound story, "The Last Demon" illus-
trates Singer's most effective use of demonology:
to dramatize moral choice by linking the demon's
defeat not to his own weakness but to his adversary's strength.

Singer's third volume of stories, *Short Friday*
(1964), signals his gradual shift to American settings. Although he abandons neither Poland nor
his characteristic mix of the real and the grotesque,
his always moral fiction takes on new dimensions
in America. Historically, Singer's Polish fiction ter-
minates in 1939 with the Nazi bombardment of
Warsaw that closes *The Family Moskat*. While the
shadow of the Holocaust lies over this fiction and
Holocaust imagery fills its pages, the ultimate disaster had not yet occurred. In postwar America,
however, Singer's Jews are mostly refugees, survivors of the Holocaust that has marked them forever. Some are, like Esther ("The Cafeteria"), the

living dead from the concentration camps; others are, like Dr. Solomon Margolin ("A Wedding in Brownsville"), the lucky few who escaped Europe undamaged. Yet even Margolin, "an important figure in Jewish circles in New York," is a victim of the malaise that affects fortunate and unfortunate alike: "Hitler's carnage and the extinction of his family had rooted out his last hope for better days, had destroyed all his faith in humanity." The hopelessness engendered by suffering and loss leads Holocaust survivors easily to one of Singer's moral conclusions—contempt for an unclean world; less easily to its corollary—faith in God's dispensation. When these survivors find themselves in America, whatever faith they retain is severely tested. Singer's aging refugees encounter in Manhattan a world in which Jewish dress and customs, the Yiddish language, and even worship itself seem barely to exist. Virtue comes to consist mainly in holding on to the crumbs of Jewishness that a dominant secular culture threatens to swallow. Understandably passive, these survivors often view themselves as the ironic remnants of a vanished way of life. A paradoxical fear arises: that the destruction of Jewry so nearly accomplished by Nazi persecution will be completed by American tolerance.

In Singer's Polish fiction the plunge into freedom is invariably disastrous. Passion, unhinged
from reason, leads to moral degradation, eventually to Gehenna. In his American fiction New
York, the ultimate symbol of freedom, becomes
Gehenna realized. Orthodox Jews find difficulty in
rounding up a *minyan* (quorum) for prayer. Blatant
sexuality corrupts relationships between men and
women. Families break down as parents and children go their separate ways, the former clinging to
the remains of a lost world, the latter assimilating
into American life. Increasingly Singer becomes
his own protagonist, sifting the detritus of modern
civilization and chronicling its failures. A thinly
veiled authorial persona largely replaces the third
person or demonic narrator of much of his earlier
fiction. Invariably a Yiddish writer of a certain age,
the narrator matches Singer's physical description.
Sometimes he occupies a story's foreground, as in
"The Mentor" or "The Son," acting as his own protagonist or sharing center stage in works that contain explicit autobiographical references. At other
times he serves primarily as a confidante, record-
ing another's story, as in "The Captive" or *The Penitent.* Whatever the specific setting or narrative
strategy of these tales of contemporary life, their
common denominator is revulsion from the mod-

ern world. As a modern man himself, the Singer who inhabits his own fiction can finally offer only limited consolations: vegetarianism as an antidote to violence; childlessness as an antidote to the suffering of innocents; hope as an antidote to despair.

Notes

1. Isaac Bashevis Singer, *In My Father's Court* (New York: Farrar, Straus, 1966) 68. Further references to this work are given in parentheses.

2. Joel Blocker and Richard Elman, "An Interview with Isaac Bashevis Singer," *Commentary*, Nov. 1963: 368.

3. Blocker and Elman 369.

4. Irving Howe, introduction, *Selected Short Stories of Isaac Bashevis Singer* (New York: Modern Library, 1966) xiv.

5. Lucy S. Dawidowicz, *The Jewish Presence: Essays on Identity and History* (New York: Harcourt Brace, 1978) 18. The Midrash consists of rabbinic commentary, notes, homilies, and stories on scriptural passages.

CHAPTER TWO

Satan in Goray
and *The Slave*

Nearly thirty years separate the composition of *Satan in Goray* in 1933 from the publication of *The Slave* in 1962. Yet these two novels of seventeenth-century Poland share many affinities of setting, theme, and treatment. Both take place in the wake of the pogrom unleashed by Bogdan Chmelnicki in 1648. Before his Cossack hordes were subdued, nearly a quarter of a million Polish and Ukrainian Jews were massacred, hundreds of Jewish settlements were destroyed, and thousands of Jews were forced to convert to Christianity. Thousands more chose martyrdom rather than relinquish their faith. The vast scale of the massacres, hitherto unprecedented in European history, threatened the very existence of East European Jewry and awakened messianic yearnings in those

Jews who survived. To these traumatized survivors only the coming of God's Messiah could rescue His chosen people from their oppressors. So when the Levantine pretender, Sabbatai Zevi, "revealed" himself as the Messiah, many despairing Jews dared to hope that the end of days was at hand and prepared to follow Zevi to Palestine. It is this period from Chmelnicki's enormities to Zevi's deception (1666) and its tragic aftermath that Singer chronicles in *Satan in Goray* and *The Slave*.

While *Satan in Goray* is a study of the effects of fanatical messianism upon an entire community, and *The Slave* is a love story in which messianism plays a relatively minor role, both novels are ultimately concerned with the moral foundations of Jewish life. Reflecting this concern, both end with short, overtly moral sections in which messianic fervor is displaced by penitential reverence. Evil, ubiquitous as ever in Singer's fiction, is located not only among the violent and primitive Gentiles of *The Slave*, but within the Jewish *shtetls* of both novels. In *Satan in Goray* the grotesque takes the form of a host of imps and demons, and a *dybbuk* (evil spirit) even occupies a human body. In *The Slave* demonology gives way to equally grotesque animal imagery; near-bestial Gentile peasants are likened to monkeys and geese, and others emit sounds of horses, dogs, and donkeys.

Satan in Goray

Satan in Goray opens on a landscape devastated by Chmelnicki's massacres. Goray, "in the midst of the hills at the end of the world," lies completely deserted, the streets littered with unburied corpses that are ravaged by savage dogs, vultures, and crows. Wild beasts lurk in the dense woods surrounding Goray, their numbers multiplied since the mass slaughter. Yet Singer's archetypal *shtetl* becomes the locus not only of despair but of hope. Years after the devastation a handful of survivors begin to return; houses are repaired, shops reopened, and economic activity resumed. The rebirth of Goray reenacts an ancient drama of Jewish survival that is symbolically capped by the return of the famous Rabbi Benish Ashkenazi, whose house and stacks of holy volumes are miraculously preserved. As life in Goray slowly revives, Rabbi Benish repeatedly thanks God for sparing a remnant of his flock. To the rabbi the horrors of 1648 were visited upon the Jews "because they had been unfaithful to the Law." That any survive at all is evidence of God's mercy and a powerful incentive for Jews to return to the ways of their fathers. It is in their failure to do so that they bring on Goray's second fall.

Hints that Goray's fragile new order will not

hold pile up in chapter 4, "The Old Goray and the New." The Goray of 1666 bears little resemblance to old Goray, where "everything had proceeded in an orderly fashion." Those were the days of easy living, presided over by Rabbi Benish, when Jewishness was held in high esteem. In the new Goray, where communal unity and responsibility have disappeared, the townspeople doze off at the rabbi's town meetings. Rabbi Benish's waning influence signals the inability of traditionalism to weld the Jewish community together. Indeed Rabbi Benish cannot unite even his own household, which has been locked in an interminable family quarrel since before 1648. Fearing the destructive power of "the sin of controversy," he has tried to mediate between his sons, the worthless Ozer and the haughty Levi, and their squabbling families. Failing to quell his unruly household and shaken in faith by the recent massacres, the aging Rabbi Benish locks himself in his room, no longer emerging even to visit his wife's bedroom on Friday nights.

Whether the rabbi's impotence is an indictment of the townspeople of Goray, of traditional Judaism, or simply of Benish himself, his decline coincides with the rise of messianic fervor in Goray. Rumors of the coming of the Messiah had already unsettled the town. With the arrival of a

rabbinical legate from Yemen bringing news of
Sabbatai Zevi, "our Messiah and holy king," the
tumult in Goray rises to fever pitch. Reb Mordecai
Joseph, a lame and fiery local cabalist and a long-
time enemy of Rabbi Benish, is apparently seized
by a vision of imminent redemption, and becomes
Zevi's staunchest advocate in Goray. Since one
version of Jewish messianism holds that the Messiah will come "when the world becomes so evil
and suffering so intense that it needs redemption
and God grants it out of His Compassion,"[1] the
survivors of the Chmelnicki slaughter may be ex-
cused for feeling that the time is at hand. Already
weakened, the fragile bonds of community snap
as traditionalists confront Sabbatians: the blood-
spattered study house is a fit symbol of a sundered
community.

With the arrival of Reb Itche Mates, a packman
less interested in peddling his wares than in extolling the virtues of Sabbatai Zevi, the messianic sect
gains a powerful new ally. According to Itche
Mates, the holy kingdom will be revealed when
Sabbatai Zevi succeeds in wresting from the
powers of darkness the "few holy sparks" that
continue to burn "among the husks of being" and
returning them to their primal source. At that moment, when bodies become pure spirit, ritual cere-
monies and even the Talmud itself would no

longer be necessary. Divulging such mysteries and seemingly familiar with "every detail of the supreme hierarchy," Itche Mates is accepted as "a holy man, truly one of the elect." His asceticism seems added evidence of his holiness: "from Sabbath to Sabbath" he lashes his body with thorns and thistles; he recites the midnight prayers only after immersing himself seventy-two times in the ritual bath; and he periodically rolls in the snow. Rabbi Benish denounces him as a "foolish zealot"; but more and more Jews, their hearts set on returning to God, flock to Itche Mates, sharing his cabalistic revelations and his asceticism.

Part 1 of *Satan in Goray* ends with the total defeat of Rabbi Benish Ashkenazi and the traditional Judaism he represents. Shattered in body and soul, he is carted off to Lublin to die. Tempting as it is to see in the rise of Itche Mates and the fall of Rabbi Benish the triumph of evil over good, this view is oversimplified. Long before Itche came on the scene, Rabbi Benish could arrest neither the drift away from communal unity nor the constant bickering in his own household. Moreover, the charge of hypocrisy leveled at Itche Mates by the Lublin letter writer is not borne out by his actions in Goray. His asceticism, no less than his belief in Zevi, seems authentic; and he makes no attempt to profit from his "revelations." In Goray there are no clearly demarcated zones of good and evil, only a climate of uncertainty. The difficulty of determining whether Sabbatai Zevi is a true Messiah is treated by Singer as an aspect of the general difficulty of separating truth from falsehood. Only after Itche Mates marries Rechele will his true nature be fully revealed.

Rechele's history is the history of Goray itself. Like the new Goray she was spawned by the massacres of 1648, the year of her birth. Blood and violence attend her upbringing in the home of her uncle Zeydel Ber, the ritual slaughterer. There she witnesses gruesome scenes of animal slaughter and suffers the persecutions of Zeydel Ber's ancient mother-in-law. Years after her death this sadistic "granny," her head covered by a bloody handkerchief, invades Rechele's dreams, terrifying the young girl into speechlessness and paralysis. Later Rechele regains her speech, "but her left leg continued paralyzed and she walked with a limp." Always sickly, she is "beset by mysterious ills" which some attribute to demonic possession. Rechele survives this first of many infernal visitations, "but from that evening on she was never the same." Permanently damaged by her *Walpurgisnacht*, Rechele is henceforth "one apart." Her unique status, combined with the facts of her birth and upbringing, underlines the importance of Rechele's role as a microcosm of the community. The demons at large in Goray inhabit her body as well. Like the new Goray she was spawned by the 1648 slaughter, and like the town she survives in an altered state. Her marriage to Itche Mates will expand her symbolic role as it exposes his.

Itche Mates spends the three days prior to wedding Rechele "in a constant round of mortifications." One the day of the wedding Rechele sits white-lipped, gazing into the distance, her face "livid and drawn as after a long illness." During the course of the wedding the fool's melancholy chant evokes the 1648 massacres in gory terms hardly appropriate for the occasion: "Chmelnicki slit open bellies, he sewed cats inside (because of our sins!)." Itche Mates, clad in "a white robe like a shroud," is led to a bridal canopy which stands between the prayer house court, where small mounds mark the graves of schoolchildren martyred in 1648, and the old cemetery. After the wedding, smelling of "bathhouse water and corpses," he goes to Rechele's bed, where his inability to consummate their marriage confirms the worst fears of the Lublin letter writer. But it is the ironic contrast between Itche's impotence and his earlier promise of fecundity that most fully defines the marriage.

At the betrothal feast there was no hint of the somberness of the wedding or of its farcical aftermath. Itche Mates, resplendent in silk caftan, "was in high spirits, his face flushed, eyes bright." In his elation he doled out brandy and spiced wine, alluded often to "the mystery of holy sexual union," and finally led the revelers in a frenzied dance. The radically different atmospheres of the bacchic betrothal feast and the funereal wedding are defined by contrasting songs. The fool's grisly evocation of Chmelnicki at the wedding bears no resemblance to the hopeful chant of Chinkele the Pious at the feast:

Protect, Lord God, this bride and groom;
May we see the Messiah soon,
The Holy Presence, Lord God wed
As these two seek the marriage bed.[2]

By juxtaposing her yearning for the Messiah and her prayer for "this bride and groom," Chinkele strongly implies their interdependence. The coming of the Messiah may well hinge upon the fulfilled potential of the sought-for marriage bed. Because he is so closely identified with Sabbatai Zevi, Itche's impotence discredits messianic asceticism if not Zevi himself. Dismayed by their leader's initial failure, the important members of the sect remind Itche Mates, "To be fruitful and to multiply is the principle of principles!" But he remains impotent during a night which, for his still-virgin bride, replicates the *Walpurgisnacht* of granny's visitation. Aware that the Angel of Death lurks outside, Rechele dreams first of "her father lying in a field, empty-eyed and circled by a flock of vultures," then of her uncle "wearing a bloody shroud" and waving a butcher's knife. Waking in the morning, she seems "altered, as though by a mysterious disease."

Itche's inability to join Rechele in "holy sexual union" constitutes a violation of the "principle of principles" and of Rechele herself. Already a symbol of the Goray community by virtue of her birth and upbringing, and her divided nature, Rechele is now forced to bear the heavier symbolic burden of Israel itself. The words of Chinkele's song evoked a scenario in which the mystical union of the Lord God and the Holy Presence would find its earthly reenactment in the marriage of Itche Mates and Rechele. According to the symbolic theology of Judaism, "God is male. Israel in relation to God is female: the Bridegroom God and the Virgin Israel. The *Shekhinah*, the Divine Presence, represents the feminine potency within God. . . . In the books of the Prophets and, of course, in the Song of Songs, marriage and sexual relations symbolize the ties between God and Israel."[3] Itche's impotence makes of Chinkele's scenario a farcical parody of the relationship between God and Israel. Asceticism in marriage is an affront to God, an implicit denial of the fullness of His identity. Part of that identity—the *Shekhinah*—lies moribund in the person of the unfulfilled Rechele. Orphaned and abused as a child, the young Rechele embodied the sufferings of Goray's Jews; violated anew as an unwilling partner in a parodic marriage, the adult Rechele embodies the sufferings of all Israel. By equating the people of Israel with an injured or abandoned woman, Singer ironically reverses the symbolic theology of Judaism. God's union with Israel dissolves into estrangement from His chosen people.

As a symbol of forsaken Israel, Rechele is redundant. Jewish history in general and the Chmelnicki massacres in particular are evidence enough. As an epitome of a critical aspect of Israel forsaken—namely Israel unredeemed—Rechele is, however, all but indispensable. Since the advent of the Messiah is related to the pangs of childbirth, her sterile marriage is the metaphorical equivalent of unredeemed Israel. In a different context Itche's asceticism would be a badge of piety. Singer's fiction is filled with men who take up asceticism as a way of life. A penitent such as Yasha Mazur (*The*

Magician of Lublin) embraces self-denial as a strategy for redeeming a misspent life. Others desert or divorce their wives in order to devote themselves to Jewishness. Such a man is seventy-five-year-old Reb Eljokum ("Strangers"), who divorces his wife with her consent, "to live out his last years in the land of Israel and to be buried on the Mount of Olives." Long ago, however, he had heeded the command "to be fruitful and to multiply"; he leaves for Israel only after marrying off his five daughters and providing for his wife. Once in Israel, Reb Eljokum even marries a young virgin, perhaps hoping for a son to say Kaddish for him. His septuagenerian friskiness is a response to the drumbeat of life that Itche Mates never feels. For penitents who have lived wrongly and for the aged who have lived wisely, asceticism is at least plausible and occasionally laudable. For those like Itche Mates who have not lived at all, it is perversion. Attempting to hasten the end of days by purifying life out of existence, Itche succeeds only in oversimplifying the Jewish messianic vision, and thereby in impoverishing Judaism itself.

Although Itche's disgrace exposes the failure of ascetic Sabbatianism, it does not undermine belief in Sabbatai Zevi himself. A far more charismatic Sabbatian than Itche appears in Goray to announce that Zevi, already revealed as the Messiah, has set out for Stamboul, "to claim the crown of the Sultan who ruled the land of Israel." The bearer of this news of imminent redemption is Reb Gedaliya, whose reputation as a cabalist is already well known to the Zevi sect. A ritual slaughterer forced to leave his native Zamosc because of his belief in Sabbatai Zevi, Reb Gedaliya is welcomed by Sabbatians and accepted even by traditionalists, since "all the people of Goray longed for meat." Such craving for flesh is invariably a harbinger of disaster in Singer's fiction. Life grows more pleasant in Goray, however, once Reb Gedaliya assumes the office of slaughterer, significantly vacant since 1648. Exuberant, sensual, luxuriously dressed, he revives the townspeople's flagging spirits and rejuvenates the Sabbatai Zevi sect, which "immediately forgot the melancholy Itche Mates, and entrusted their leadership to Reb Gedaliya."

The rise of Reb Gedaliya at the expense of Itche Mates recalls Itche's rise at the expense of Rabbi Benish. Gedaliya exploits Itche's failure to sustain the ascetic vision of the Messiah much as Itche had exploited Rabbi Benish's failure to unite the community under the banner of traditional Judaism. Although Levi heads the Sabbatai Zevi sect and holds the rabbinical chair deserted by his father, his role as the leader of Goray is soon usurped by the dynamic Reb Gedaliya. The diminished role of the rabbi plus the facts that Levi, the younger of Rabbi Benish's sons, inherited his father's office in the first place and is, moreover, a Sabbatian are symptomatic of the disorder that has plagued Goray since 1648. Only from a traditional point of view, however, is Gedaliya's new order suspect; and even the orthodox soon rally behind him as they never had behind Rabbi Benish or Itche Mates. And his appeal is understandable. Serving God through joy and hating sadness, loving rich food and clothing, drinking and dancing, Reb Gedaliya preaches devotion to the body. Not by the mortification of the flesh, but by its indulgence, will the end of history and the coming of the Messiah be hastened.

Gedaliya's pleasure principle, like Itche's asceticism, is expressed not only in public advocacy but in a private relationship. Again Rechele provides the symbolic litmus test of messianic vision. Indeed her sporadic reappearances in conjunction with the rise and fall of the town's leaders do much to establish the rhythm and tone of *Satan in Goray*. On Rechele's body and soul are imprinted the results of her community's various strivings for redemption. Having already tasted the frustrations of Itche's asceticism, she experiences the sterile lust of her seducer, Gedaliya. Whether as a result of her first mating with Gedaliya, of her habitual near-hysteria, or simply of the feverish messianic climate around her, Rechele hears the "awesome voice" of the Angel Sandalfon announcing the coming of the Messiah. Since the angel not only confirms Gedaliya's prediction but declares him a saint as well, Gedaliya enthusiastically proclaims Rechele a true prophetess inspired by the "Divine Presence." Opportunistically, he sends Itche Mates off with Mordecai Joseph to spread the news, at one stroke securing dominance over Rechele and Goray.

Under Gedaliya's dispensation "Goray, that small town at the edge of the world was altered. No one recognized it any longer" (166). The notoriety of Gedaliya and Rechele, that "holy pair," makes Goray the goal of pilgrims seeking miraculous cures, but also of beggars, vagabonds, and social misfits who live by begging from the pilgrims. The marriage of two beggars on a dung hill epitomizes the newly prosperous Goray; in the flouting of a crucial Jewish sacrament it prefigures the spreading communal stain. As the constraints that define Jewishness fall away, relationships between the sexes are perverted. Adultery, wifeswapping, adolescent pregnancy, and homosexuality flourish in a climate grown so liberal that even ritual and dietary laws are disregarded. Again Rechele serves as a microcosm of her disordered community, this time in her illicit union with Gedaliya. Naked, he approaches her bed, "a thick growth of hair covering his body like a fur coat" (176). Animalistic in his lust, Gedaliya is described in the same language applied to Reb Simon, whose marriage to Hindele gives "The Black Wedding" its ominous title. When Itche Mates and Mordecai Joseph return with the shattering news of Sabbatai Zevi's conversion to Islam, the triumph of the "Evil One" in Goray seems complete.

Exposing the false messiah, however, does not lay the messianic controversy to rest. On the contrary, the exposure of Zevi causes a ripple effect that spreads the stain of Goray's corruption as it widens the scope of Singer's treatment of the phenomenon of Jewish messianism. In the wake of Gedaliya's explanation that only "Sabbatai Zevi's shadow was converted," many "abandoned the Faithful," joining Mordecai Joseph in doing penance "for having succumbed to the seduction of the false redeemer." The remaining faithful split into competing factions, one asserting "that the Messiah would not appear until the generation had become completely virtuous," the other arguing that "the generation before redemption had to become completely guilty" (197). The fractured Jewish community of Goray becomes emblematic of the dissension that racks "every Jewish settlement" from Vilna to Jerusalem and drives Jews to baptism or to suicide. To round off the symbolic design of *Satan in Goray,* Singer, as usual, reenacts the trials of the community upon the body of Rechele. Married at last to Gedaliya, whose failure to wait the legal ninety days after her divorce from Itche Mates marks his open "contempt for the Talmud," Rechele no longer hears the "holy angels" who spoke to her before Sabbatai Zevi's apostasy. Her wasted body becomes a battleground upon which the sacred—"like Rabbi Benish in the old days"—and the profane wage war. Their battle culminates in her rape and impregnation by Satan, whose total possession of Rechele signals the definitive victory of evil in Goray. Totally debilitated, visited daily by fresh catastrophes, Goray is finally the graveyard of messianic yearnings.

With the symbolic death of Goray the narrative proper concludes. For Singer, however, moral interpretation defies narrative closure. In order to explore fully the moral reverberations of his tale, Singer grafts upon it two chapters excerpted from a book of moral instruction—*The Works of the Earth.* Written long after the events it recapitulates in a quasi-biblical style, the appended narrative is an overtly didactic attempt to justify God's ways in language comprehensible even to "women, and girls and common folk." To the end of convincing his readers to return to God's ways, the narrator abandons the detached and objective tone of the main body of the novel for one of absolute moral judgment. Characters and issues once ambiguous are clarified: Rabbi Benish is of sainted memory, Gedaliya of the devil's party; Sabbatai Zevi was a false messiah, his worship heretical. Singer's coda ends in an explicit statement of its lesson:

LET NONE ATTEMPT TO FORCE THE LORD: TO END OUR PAIN WITHIN THE WORLD: THE MESSIAH WILL COME IN GOD'S OWN TIME (239).

Not only in its condemnation of messianic zeal but in its implied hatred of all zealotry, the homily announces one of Singer's recurring convictions: that excess breeds chaos.

For Singer the distorted messianism that takes the form of fanatical zeal leads only to the sundering of the Jewish community, the metaphorical equivalent of anarchy. While messianic yearning is a plausible psychological response to suffering, it becomes sinful when it contravenes Jewish moral law, thereby provoking more of the very suffering it seeks to transcend. By recalling 1648, by branding Goray "an accursed town," and by describing Gedaliya's eventual apostasy in language fit for Chmelnicki, Singer implies that the destruction of the Jewish community can come as easily from

within as without. In the short story aptly titled
"Errors" (1975) he alludes to the followers of Sabbatai Zevi in terms reminiscent of *Satan in Goray:*
"Members of this sect believed that the Messiah
would come either when all was pure or all corruption. They caused Jews to sin." Satan, the narrator of "The Destruction of Kreshev," credits "the
power of a false cabalist and the corrupt words of a
disciple of Sabbatai Zevi," a latter-day Gedaliya,
with visiting upon Kreshev the identical plagues
that rained down upon Goray. One of Singer's
most harrowing stories, "The Destruction of
Kreshev" was published in the 1943 volume that
featured the reissued *Satan in Goray.* Again in *The
Slave* messianic fervor engenders evil and division
in a Jewish *shtetl* contemporaneous with Goray;
and even in novels set a century or two later, messianic zealotry persists, albeit in the modern guise
of yearning for political utopia.

But perhaps the most striking evidence of
Singer's fascination with the messianic theme occurs in *Der Zindiker Meshiekh: Historisher Roman*
(*The Sinning Messiah: A Historical Novel*). Serialized
in the Forward beginning in October 1935, but
never translated, this novel remains virtually unknown to anglophone readers and unmentioned
by its author.[4] Yet it is significant that for his first
extended fiction after *Satan in Goray,* a work that

ended a two-year creative hiatus and effectively introduced him to Yiddish-American readers, Singer returned to the false messiah. *The Sinning Messiah* repeatedly invokes the name and career of Sabbatai Zevi, still notorious to Jews nearly a century after his death. Set in eighteenth-century Bucharest, the novel tells of Jacob Frank, the last of the quasi-messiahs, whose repudiation of the Talmud, indulgence in orgies, and eventual conversion eerily parallel the actions of Gedaliya in *Satan in Goray*. Tracing the evil and divisiveness attendant upon false messianism, *The Sinning Messiah* recapitulates the moral of its predecessor. Singer had already found in the false messiah a powerful objective correlative for his distrust of excess. Relevant to nearly all of his later fiction is the belief stated in the title story ("The Image") of his most recent collection by one of his most revered narrators, Aunt Yentl: "Everything that is exaggerated does damage."

Aunt Yentl's words amplify the didactic conclusion of *Satan in Goray*. And the novel yields its richest meaning when her message is embellished by another lesson embedded in *The Works of the Earth* and valued equally by Singer: the virtue of repentance. Itche Mates and Mordecai Joseph were, like Gadaliya, fanatical messianists whose devotion to the cabala marked the excessive zealotry denounced by Rabbi Benish. Their evident contrition, however, has the effect of morally distancing Mordecai Joseph and Itche Mates from the unregenerate Gedaliya, although they share with him the responsibility for corrupting Goray. In *The Works of the Earth*, Mordecai Joseph, whose penance "had saved his soul," becomes a hero, exorcising from Rechele the *dybbuk* which had entered her body with Satan's violation. Three days after the *dybbuk's* departure Rechele dies, her strength having been sustained only by the evil spirit within her. Her death provides the occasion for the redemption of Itche Mates, who "mourned her and recited the Mourner's Prayer over her grave." The reclamation of this husband and no husband is climaxed by his death from a broken heart. Before dying, "he bade that he be buried near her: And thus that righteous man passed away with a kiss" (238). Perhaps it is significant that Rechele's body, the repository of individual and communal guilt, should be the locus of Mordecai Joseph's exorcism and Itche's mourning, both acts of penitential virtue. In the former's heroic struggle with the *dybbuk*, no less than in the latter's astonishing rehabilitation, Singer evokes the saving grace of repentance. Much of his later fiction will retain this powerful coupling of false messianism and penitence, first welded together in *Satan in Goray.*

The Slave

Satan in Goray establishes the pattern of deviance and penitence so crucial to Singer's fiction. Traditional Judaism invariably defines his moral norm, false messianism his mode of deviance, penitence his return to grace. *The Slave* retains the brand of false messianism exploited in *Satan in Goray*. Its hero, Jacob, succumbs temporarily to the Sabbatian heresy and dies a penitent. Jacob's is a tortuous and circuitous path to redemption, however, precisely because Sabbatianism is but one among the many temptations he must withstand. Only near the end of *The Slave* is Sabbatai Zevi invoked as the epitome of the last evil to be overcome. The erring Jews of *Satan in Goray* invite chaos by casting off the yoke of traditional Judaism for the ostensible freedom of false messianism. Of course the freedom they exercise is as one dimensional as it is specious: messianism seems the sole outlet to a desperate and frightened people. By multiplying the possibilities and ambiguities of freedom, Singer constitutes *The Slave* as a debate about freedom itself. To this end he retains the historical background of *Satan in Goray* but radically expands its geography. A study of the effects of mass hysteria upon a community, *Satan in Goray* takes place entirely within the *shtetl*. *The Slave* is a quasi-picaresque novel which employs the Chmelnicki massacre as a device for uprooting its hero from his *shtetl* and propelling him unwillingly into the world. Bereft of family and community, Jacob struggles first to maintain his Jewish identity in an alien environment, then to rejoin the Jewish community, and finally to attain the full ripeness of Jewish life. The novel's three divisions corre-spond roughly to the various stages of its hero's struggles and of the love story that determines the form these struggles take.

"Every story is a love story," Singer is fond of repeating.[5] In *The Slave*, Jacob's love for Wanda vies initially with his love of Jewishness; the reconcilia-tion of his two loves and their eventual conver-gence into one claims much of the novel's space. At first Jacob regards his longing for Wanda as evi-dence of an impure heart. Although she has re-peatedly saved his life and "assisted him in fulfilling his obligations as a Jew," Wanda is identi-fied with the Gentile world of his persecutors. Yet Singer takes great pains to differentiate Wanda from her fellow Gentiles. Nicknamed "The Lady" by the savage Polish peasants, she is associated with the Edenic landscape of *The Slave*. Nowhere else in his fiction does Singer lavish such praise on the natural world: "Every sunrise in the moun-tains was like a miracle; one clearly discerned

God's hand among the flaming clouds."[6] On the mountainside where he tends Bzik's cows, Jacob, "solitary here as the original Adam" (135), awaits his Eve: Wanda's "body exuded the warmth of the sun, the breezes of summer" (71). Before Jacob finally succumbs, and they make love for the first time, Wanda assumes the role of a Jewess. She follows him to a freezing stream in which she performs the ritual ablutions required of Jewish women before intercourse and from which she emerges clinging to Jacob "as if undergoing martyrdom" (67). Her love for Judaism, already apparent as an implicit condition for releasing Jacob's love, is made explicit after their first lovemaking in words that echo the biblical Ruth's: "Where thou goest, I go. Thy people are my people. Thy God is my God."

The consummation of their love magnifies its ambiguities. Even in the afterglow of their first ecstasy Jacob fears that he has "forfeited the world beyond" and that his Jewishness, while still intact, has been severely compromised. With Wanda he relives Adam's first joy at the dawn of creation, in sensual delights he had never known with his wife, the "frigid and cold" Zelda. But the idyllic pastoral world of their love trysts is also inhabited by primordial peasants, "grunting like pigs, licking the earth, babbling to rocks." In their savagery and abandonment they devour the flesh of living animals and copulate so randomly that the lineage of their many bastards is unknown. Jews habitually distrust nature, which they associate with that freedom from restraint so alien to Judaism and so devastating for Jews in its wilder aspects. Beyond Wanda lies not only the wonder of natural creation but the horror of its primeval savagery.

Jacob's sexual liberation invokes the nirvana of self-fulfillment toward which so much of modern fiction drives. *The Slave* derives its tension, however, from Singer's characteristic refusal to accept the unqualified value of freedom. Intimations that Jacob's love for Wanda is a form of captivity potentially more shackling than his actual slavery attend their more and more frequent meetings. After living with Wanda for weeks, Jacob still calls their relationship "his transgression." His thoughts, once fixed upon clinging to his Jewishness, lurch out of control. Changed so drastically that he sometimes "didn't recognize himself," he even forgets, or fails to concentrate upon, his prayers. As his lust intensifies, his mother and father vanish from his dreams, displaced by visions of Wanda. Condemning Jacob's "slavery," however, is as simplistic as extolling his "freedom." Seemingly debilitated by his love for Wanda, Jacob's Jewishness is rejuvenated by her love for him. Indeed, their mutual attraction is powerfully justified by evidence that Wanda's love for Jacob is inseparable from her love for his Jewishness: "She lusted for knowledge almost as fiercely as she did for the flesh" (83). A slave to Judaism as well as to her lover, Wanda begs Jacob for instruction in Jewish beliefs and in the Yiddish language. As her two passions grow more and more indistinguishable, two formerly antithetical images converge. Shaken by her father's sudden death, Wanda cries out to Jacob "as had his mother . . . preparing for Yom Kippur Eve." The Wanda who had once displaced his parents in Jacob's dreams, and who had first seduced him before Yom Kippur, has attained full identification with is revered mother and with the holiest day of the Jewish year. It is further significant that Wanda's outcry, which triggers her conflation with sacred memory, follows immediately upon Jacob's "Well, we are all slaves . . . God's slaves" (90).

Jacob has affirmed his slavery to God amid surroundings hardly conducive to Jewish worship. Lacking "prayer shawl and phylacteries, fringed garment or holy book" (6), he had nevertheless "refused to forsake the Jewish faith" and had resisted the Gentiles' pressures to convert, along with their unclean meat. His steadfastness is symbolized by his attempt, in conscious imitation of Moses, to scratch the 613 laws on a stone that "had

THE SLAVE

been waiting ever since creation" (39). When Jacob is miraculously ransomed by his fellow Jews and taken back to Josefov, his return to the Jewish community seems the promised end of his struggle to maintain his faith. Yet this first of Jacob's several returns is not free of the ambiguity that pervades *The Slave*. The ravaged Josefov bears little resemblance to the village Jacob knew. Such Jewish landmarks as the synagogue, the study house, the ritual bath, and the poorhouse are no more, and the "murderers had even torn up the tombstones." Most significantly, Josefov is now "inhabited by fools, cripples, and madmen" (102), figures eerily reminiscent of Jacob's grotesque Gentile captors. Among the mad is his sister Miriam, reduced to recounting endlessly the horrors inflicted on the family dead. Jacob's reaction to her litany of atrocities is described in phrases generally reserved for the Holocaust: "a limit to what the human mind could accept"; "beyond the power of any man to contemplate"; "Poland . . . one vast cemetery" (106–8). And like many Holocaust survivors, he finds himself no longer able to love a God who permitted the slaughter. Jacob's faith has weathered isolation and exile only to be shaken in his native village among his own people. Exhausted by his struggle to regain the love for God he once took for granted, Jacob "had lost his taste for Torah and prayer." Wanda haunts his dreams, asking why he made her a Jew only to leave her "among the idolators." That congruence of sacred and profane loves, so hard won by Jacob in captivity, dissolves in Josefov. With its dissolution Jacob, tortured by his betrayal of both God and Wanda, relives the darkest days of his exile. Sitting forlorn in the study house, "longing for the open air" and Wanda, "he remained a slave. Passion held him like a dog on a leash" (113).

Jacob's nostalgia for his slavery is fueled by his failure not only to fathom God's way, but to understand man's. Appalled by God's seeming indifference to His martyred people, Jacob is no less appalled by his fellow Jews, who "had learned nothing from their ordeal; rather suffering had pushed them lower" (119). Freed from a primitive and savage peasantry whose lawlessness was predictable, Jacob finds himself in a Jewish community that "observed the laws and customs involving the Almighty, but broke the code regulating man's treatment of man with impunity" (117). Under the terms of this indictment Jews fare little better than their Gentile oppressors. The theme of man's inhumanity to man, pervasive in post-Holocaust Jewish literature, is invariably employed as a condemnation of Nazi atrocities. By invoking it in *The Slave*, Singer indicts not only the

strict observance of Jewish halachic law as an end
in itself, but the convenient substitution of a set of
narrow regulations for human obligations. Elie
Wiesel, himself a Holocaust survivor, tells of an
Israeli rabbi, well known for his "intolerance in religious matters," who nonetheless "permitted his
disciples to dig trenches on the Sabbath: 'To abandon man is more serious a sin than to abandon
God,' he told them."[7] Jacob, whose "love for the
Jews had been whole-hearted when he was distant
from them," despises their barbed tongues and
their petty stratagems and quarrels when among
them. Crestfallen, he flees Josefov for Lublin, only
to be further disillusioned by "the attitude of the
Jews who, having just survived their greatest ca-
lamity, behaved as if they no longer remembered."
Again, a post-Holocaust dictum—the sacred duty
of remembrance—is invoked to castigate the errant
Jews of *The Slave.* Disheartened by his coreligion-
ists and miserable among them, Jacob passes "beyond freedom," back to the scene of his slavery
and to Wanda.

    When Jacob rejoins Wanda at the end of part 1
of the novel, he takes up a burden now grown
heavier: "His years of enforced slavery had been
succeeded by a slavery that would last as long as
he lived" (159). Yet slavery is preferable to the vari-
eties of anarchic freedom he encounters in part 2.

When Jacob and Wanda—now Sarah, the name given to Jewish converts—settle as man and wife in Pilitz, they enter a Jewish community more debased than that in Josefov. Pilitz is run by Gershon, who levies confiscatory taxes on all but his friends and flatterers, who places his sons-in-law in the town's most influential positions, who charges exorbitant prices for graves, and whose contempt for his fellowman and his community is so great that he indulges himself in mid-week steam baths, forcing the bath attendant "to heat the water at the community's expense." The same contempt surfaces in Sarah's treatment at the hands of Pilitz's Jewish women. Fearing that her poor Yiddish will betray her Gentile birth, Sarah pretends to be mute, thereby exposing herself to the women's ridicule. Added to Gershon's ignorance and corruption, their cruel mockery of "Dumb Sarah" deepens the novel's indictment of communal Judaism. Like the Jews of Josefov and Lublin, those of Pilitz strictly observe minor rituals and customs, wanting "to be kind to God and not to man" (219). Part 2 of *The Slave* is punctuated by Jacob's sighs of despair over the actions of his fellow Jews. At one point he attributes the Messiah's delay, the length of the Jewish exile, and even the Chmelnicki massacres to Jewish sinfulness. And finally, after Sarah's death and the elders' refusal to inter her in the cemetery, Jacob "understood his religion: its essence was the relation between man and his fellows. Man's obligations toward God were easy to perform" (247). In their refusal to accept Sarah—living or dead—lies the harshest judgment on the Jews of Pilitz.

Gershon and his cohorts use their freedom to abuse that of others. Their treatment of Sarah, a stranger in their midst, is little better than Jacob's at the hands of his Polish overseers. Indeed, Jan Bzik regarded Jacob as a son, and the peasants offered the slave equal status among them should he convert. In the context of their savagery, the peasants' offer is magnanimous; and it shames the Jewish elders who deny Sarah's conversion and her right to burial. Lest it appear, however, that Christians are any better than Jews, Lord and Lady Pilitzky are presented as the ultimate abusers of freedom. Devout Christians, whose endless debaucheries are relieved by periods of intense mortification, the Pilitzkys epitomize the degeneration of the Polish nobility. Their sexual infidelities— "She watched him corrupt peasant girls and he eavesdropped on her and her lovers" (176)—recall the licentious couplings of the Polish peasants but without the excuse of the peasants' primitive ignorance. Displays of hunting trophies and weapons are reminders of the means by which the Pilitzkys won their status and maintain it: "The very air of the castle smelled of violence, idolatry, and concupiscence." Adam Pilitzky sees in Jewish suffering the evidence that Christians have displaced Jews as God's chosen people. In that very suffering, however, lies the best evidence for preferring even the debased Judaism of Pilitz to the Christianity of the Pilitzkys: rather fall with the murdered than triumph with the murderers.

The various Jewish and Christian abuses of freedom throw the virtuous slavery of Jacob and Sarah into high relief. Because Polish law decrees the death penalty for any Christian who converts to Judaism, they live in constant fear that her Gentile origins will be discovered. Jacob and Sarah are slaves: he to his guilt for his liaison with a Gentile, she to silence and derision, both to their mutual love and to God. In part due to the failings of Pilitz's Jews, in part to her own piety and goodness, Sarah appears to Jacob as "really a saint, a thousand times better than any of the others" (239). On the eve of Yom Kippur he concludes that "she should omit that part of the prayer where the names of the dead are mentioned. For she, Sarah, had not been orphaned through the death of Jan Bzik. Her real father was the patriarch Abraham" (217). Sarah, in death, is a "Holy Soul": Jacob "watched over the body of a saint" (244). While

Sarah's saintliness is no proof against the malice of the Jewish elders who refuse her burial, it confirms her link to a covenantal Judaism far removed from the narrow legalism of the Pilitz community. For Sarah's is the pure, biblical Judaism taught her by Jacob and practiced with him among Jews and Gentiles alike. Born with "a Jewish soul," the "martyred Sarah, who had estranged herself from both Jews and gentiles, and lost her home and language" (244), gains full identification with her biblical namesake, the mother of the Jews.

Sarah's apotheosis as Jewish icon climaxes in her difficult pregnancy and subsequent death. So severe are her labor pains that "Dumb Sarah" cries out in Polish, at one stroke denying her muteness and revealing her Gentile origins. When she screams, "Where's Jacob? . . . Has he forgotten his Wanda?" (226) the credulous women at her bedside conclude that a Gentile *dybbuk* named Wanda has invaded Sarah's body. Quite unlike the "real" *dybbuk*, a straightforward embodiment of evil, that possessed Rechele in *Satan in Goray*, the *dybbuk* conjured up by the Jewish harpies of *The Slave* is none other then Wanda, who embodies the goodness and beauty of the natural world. Singer ironically reverses the *dybbuk's* normal attributes in order to unite in Wanda-Sarah the hitherto unresolved dualities of nature and religion. Sarah's death, shortly after giving birth to a son, is in a sense anticlimactic. True, it exposes the hypocrisy of the Jewish elders, thereby prompting Jacob to see in human relationships the essence of Judaism. But the failings of *shtetl* Judaism had evoked a similar response from Jacob as long ago as Josefov. Not in death, but in the prolonged agony of her pregnancy, Sarah completed her symbolic transformation into her biblical counterpart. While the purified Judaism that she finally embodies is that which Jacob taught and to which he yearns to return, the dualities symbolically fused in Wanda-Sarah remain unresolved in Jacob.

After Sarah's death the vital interplay between freedom and slavery intensifies. Numbed by personal tragedy and communal perfidy, Jacob is torn from his vigil over the still unburied Sarah by Polish soldiers come to arrest him for the crime of converting a Christian. Even after breaking from his captors and prying off and burying the chain that dangles from his wrist, Jacob remains dazed and purposeless. Overcome by exhaustion, he falls into "the deep sleep of those who have ceased to hope. Each time he woke, he wondered, Where am I running? Why did I escape?" (255). Yet the very act of escape is an affirmation of life; and the buried chain is a powerful symbol of freedom, no matter how circumscribed. Moreover, Jacob's sudden burst of energy signals the end of a passivity no less apparent for its being forced upon him. From years of slavery through years of clandestine marriage, Jacob's life has been dictated largely by circumstances. Animated by the same life force that once drove him back to Wanda, his escape at least indicates the will to take control of his own destiny. Although freedom initially strikes Jacob as meaningless, it offers the potential for self-determination. It remains for Jacob to give meaning to his freedom by exercising it wisely.

In *The Slave* freedom is too often equated with license. Polish peasants and Jewish elders, Pilitzky and Gershon—all exercise the anarchic freedom that abuses others and invites chaos. Such freedom is illusory, mere enslavement to the appetites; true freedom originates in curbing the appetites and ends in slavery to God. Desiring always to serve God, but uncertain of how best to do so, Jacob had allowed his love for Wanda to govern his actions. At decisive moments in his life this dependence took the form of her appearance in his dreams. Since her image displaced thoughts of God, Jacob saw in his dependence the same surrender to appetite that motivates Pilitzky and Gershon. But the woman who fills his latest dreams embodies the convergence of profane and sacred love: "He was with her again; but now she was both Wanda and Sarah; Sarah-Wanda he called her, amazed at the coupling of these names" (253). To his plea for guidance she replies, "Fear not, Jacob my slave. . . . Go with the child . . . to the other side of the Vistula" (254). Invested with the holiness of Sarah-Wanda, these words constitute a sacred obligation. Before meeting it, however, Jacob must refuse the bait of another false freedom, perhaps the most seductive of all.

At the shore of the Vistula, Jacob encounters Waclaw, the Gentile ferryman, who unhesitatingly shares his meager food and hut with a man he recognizes as a Jew and senses to be a fugitive. Waclaw claims to be "free as a bird," precisely because he acknowledges no responsibility to God or man. An atheist, he can neither serve an unseen God nor accept the "rope around my neck" of marriage or property or community. To Jacob, whose experience confirms Waclaw's theory that human relationships are most often enslaving or corrupting, the ferryman's independence is tantalizing. When Jacob insists that "men cannot be entirely free," that someone must raise crops and children, Waclaw counters with, "Let the others do it." While he accepts the argument that man's "every desire is a strand of rope that yokes him," Jacob is saved from the nihilism inherent in Waclaw's position by his slavery to God. As a father

Jacob cannot disclaim responsibility for his son, "who must grow up instructed in the Torah." By assigning the role of devil's advocate to a ferryman, Singer lays the symbolic groundwork for Jacob's moral choice: To board the ferry without his son is to secure only the empty freedom awaiting him across the Vistula.

Jacob's refusal to abandon his son as the price of "freedom" is in itself merely a species of negative virtue. To prod him into action Singer produces a white-bearded Jew, an emissary from the Holy Land who Jacob "knew . . . had been sent to him." The emissary plays the role previously filled by Sarah in Jacob's dreams, repeating her message: "You must save yourself and you must save the child" (266), and expanding it in a specifically Jewish context. The old man passes judgment on Jacob and resolves the ambiguities of his relationship with Sarah: "The community is right. Your wife was a gentile and so is your son. The child follows its mother. This is the law. But behind the law, there is mercy. Without mercy, there would be no law" (265). To save the child—and himself—Jacob must reclaim his son for Judaism. Inspired by the emissary's words and emboldened by his recent escape from the soldiers, which links him to the ancient heroes of the Bible rather than to the Jews who passively yielded to their butchers, Jacob steals back into Pilitz. By returning to the scene of his wife's death and his son's birth, Jacob repeats the earlier pattern of his wanderings. But the Jacob who prostrates himself upon the fresh mound of Sarah's grave, then vows to atone for his sins, is a new man. No longer indecisive, his destiny clear, Jacob passes beyond slavery to the senses into the pure realm of slavery to God: "For the rest of his life and until his last breath, he must repent and ask forgiveness of God and of Sarah's sacred soul" (272). As if contingent upon his self-purification, Jacob's escape from Pilitz with his son is easily accomplished. Weeping and singing for joy, the purified Jacob is clearly under God's protection. Bathed in a "strange light that flooded the forest" and illumines his way to the Vistula, Jacob is inspired to name his son Ben-oni (Benjamin), "a child born of sorrow." As father and son near the ferry crossing, the "river's calmness, purity and radiance" attest to the beauty of creation and prompt Jacob to renew his promise of servitude to its author: "Lead, God, lead. It is thy world" (279).

Jacob's reaffirmation, which concludes part 2 of *The Slave*, seems to complete the passage from sin to redemption that leads Singer's most sympathetic heroes back to God. Although Singer's biblical analogies are inconsistent, Jacob appears to have gained the full identification with his biblical namesake previously achieved by Sarah with hers. Wanda-Sarah was Ruth in her devotion to the Jewish people and their God; Rachel as the wife, beloved and lost, of Jacob; and finally Sarah as Jewish convert and mother. Jacob has been variously likened to Moses (scratching commandments in stone); to Joseph in Egypt (slave among the Gentiles; refusing Lady Pilitzky's sexual advances); but most often to Jacob the patriarch. Waiting for the ferry, he recalls the biblical Jacob, who also "lost a beloved wife, the daughter of an idolator, among strangers" (278); who was left with a son; and who crossed the river carrying only a staff, pursued by Esau. Despite this confusion, or perhaps because of it, Singer has succeeded, by associating Sarah and Jacob with a wide range of biblical counterparts, in forging their links to the Jewish past. On the bank of the Vistula, Jacob slips effortlessly into the stream of Jewish history: "Everything remained the same: the ancient love, the ancient grief. Perhaps four thousand years would again pass; somewhere, at another river, another Jacob would walk mourning another Rachel. Or who knew, perhaps it was always the same Jacob and the same Rachel" (279).

As in *Satan in Goray*, however, Singer cannot resist the temptation to project his theme into the future. Whatever its aesthetic justification, the

short final section ("The Return") picks up the trail
of Jacob's destiny which ended satisfactorily
enough at the Vistula and follows it to his death.
Although the white-bearded emissary turned out
to be a disciple of Sabbatai Zevi who drew Jacob to
Israel for the wrong reason, Jacob has succeeded in
raising his son as a Jew. Indeed, Benjamin has become a sort of super-Jew—at twenty an instructor
in a yeshiva and the son-in-law of a rabbi—who
epitomizes his father's bonding to the Jewish future as well as to its past. Like Jacob's life in Israel
and Benjamin himself, Jacob's second return to Pilitz represents an actualization of the career he
outlined for himself twenty years earlier just before reclaiming his infant son. Barely over fifty, if
the chronology of Singer's main narrative is to be
credited, Jacob is already a white-bearded patriarch, his holy status confirmed by his penitential
labors in Israel: "He took the most difficult tasks
upon himself, carried the paralyzed, cleansed the
lice-infested sick" (297). This saint, acclaimed by
the pious as "one of the twenty-six men who are
the pillars of the world" (297), has returned to dis-
inter Sarah's body, eventually to rebury it in Israel,
on the sacred Mount of Olives. Unable to find her
unmarked grave among the many, Jacob grows
weary, and suddenly sickens and dies. Sarah's
gravesite, formerly unhallowed ground, had been

overtaken by the expansion of the original cemetery so that, ironically, her remains now mingle
with those of the Pilitz Jews who once rejected her.
Breaking ground for Jacob's burial, the gravedigger
strikes the bones of a partly decomposed body,
soon identified as Sarah's by its lack of a proper
shroud and by the strands of blond hair still en-
twined about the skull. This last image, hauntingly
reminiscent of John Donne's "The Relic," has the
same effect of sanctifying profane love, and is
rightly interpreted as evidence of God's wish that
Jacob and Sarah rest together.

Jacob's second return to Pilitz and his subsequent death reenact Singer's version of the eternal
return. Already linked to the Jewish future
through Benjamin, to the Jewish past through
Sarah and his biblical namesake, and to both past
and future through his life in Israel, symbolized by
his pouch of soil from the Holy Land, Jacob now
reforges his link to the Jewish community he once
abandoned. That this is as necessary to Singer's
scheme as it is unforeseen by Jacob was apparent
in Israel when even Benjamin had admonished
him for holding himself too aloof from his fellow
Jews. Wishing only to be buried next to Sarah on
the Mount of Olives, Jacob rests with her instead
in the Pilitz cemetery. And Pilitz, once riven and
still unsettled by Sabbatian heresy, is reunited in

communal awe of the miracle of his burial. Jacob had done sufficient penance in Israel for whatever sin he committed in living with a Gentile; his arduous return to Pilitz and to the Jewish community, as well as his sudden death, can be read as the culmination of a last penance dictated by his flirtation with Sabbatianism and by his failure to integrate himself fully into Jewish life in Israel. "The Return" has the additional function of rendering palpable God's hand in human affairs. Jacob's love for Wanda, like his removal to Israel at the behest of the Sabbatian envoy, has gained sanctification through his service to a merciful God. By following the trail that ends in Jacob's death, "The Return" provides the ultimate conclusion to Singer's familiar interplay of deviance and penitence. And as Jacob's last and most profound passage beyond freedom to slavery achieves its final destination, the miracle of his reunion with Sarah is proof positive of God's handiwork and of the transcendent virtue of serving Him which is the lesson of *The Slave.*

Notes

1. Irving H. Buchen, *Isaac Bashevis Singer and the Eternal Past* (New York: New York University Press, 1968) 88.

THE SLAVE

2. Isaac Bashevis Singer, *Satan in Goray* (New York: Noonday Press, 1955) 100. Page numbers in parentheses are to this edition.

3. Lucy S. Dawidowicz, *The Jewish Presence: Essays on Identity and History* (New York: Harcourt Brace, 1978) 50.

4. David Neal Miller, *Fear of Fiction: Narrative Strategies in the Works of Isaac Bashevis Singer* (Albany: State University of New York Press, 1985) 27, 29.

5. Paul Kresh, *Isaac Bashevis Singer: The Magician of West 86th Street* (New York: Dial, 1979) 263.

6. Singer, *The Slave* (New York: Farrar, Straus, 1962). Page references in parentheses are to this edition.

7. Elie Wiesel, *A Beggar in Jerusalem* (New York: Random House, 1970) 116.

CHAPTER THREE

The Family Moskat; The Manor and *The Estate*

The seventeenth-century Poland of *Satan in Goray* and *The Slave* is the chronological starting point for Singer's successive re-creations of the vanished world of East European Jewry. Shuttling back and forth between historical epochs, his fiction eventually spans that period from the mid-nineteenth century, when Jews began tentatively emerging from *shtetls* hardly different from Goray or Pilitz, to the late twentieth century, when America has become the haven for Holocaust survivors. Because the psychological no less than the geographical mileage from *shtetl* to city is so great, Singer expands his fiction to take in the widening scope of Jewish life. Thus, *The Family Moskat*, his first novel to be written in the United States, was serialized for three years (1945–1948) in the Jewish daily *Forward* and comprised two volumes in its original Yiddish edition (1950). *The Manor* is even longer, running to nearly 2,000 manuscript pages. Begun in 1952 and serialized in the *Forward* from 1953 to 1955, it was eventually published in English in two parts: *The Manor* and *The Estate.*

While the growing importance of the Jew on the stage of world history might justify novels of such epic proportion, Singer may have been drawn to his subject, and the consequent radical departure from the style of *Satan in Goray,* by the example of his elder brother. Both *The Family Moskat* and the one-volume reissue (1979) of *The Manor* are dedicated to I. J. Singer, "my brother . . . and master." And both novels share marked affinities with the elder Singer's masterpiece, *The Brothers Ashkenazi* (1936), a work cited specifically in *The Family Moskat* dedication. It may be simplistic to argue that *The Family Moskat* was conceived as a homage to Israel Joshua, much less as a continuation of his work. Yet Singer had been unable to publish a second novel during the decade between *Satan in Goray* and his brother's death in 1944: "the greatest misfortune of my entire life. He was my father, my teacher. I never really recovered from this blow. There was only one consolation—whatever would happen later would never be as bad as this."[1] Begun in the following year, *The Family Moskat* took the shape of the expansive family chronicle popularized in Yiddish by *The Brothers Ashkenazi*.

The Family Moskat

The spacious design of *The Family Moskat* accommodates the many characters, the interwoven plots, and the groupings of social and religious forces that also fill the pages of *The Brothers Ashkenazi*. Such densely populated fictions—Singer prefaces *The Family Moskat* with several pages detailing the complex genealogies of the Moskat, Bannet, Katzenellenbogen, and Berman families—recall also the massive family chronicles of the nineteenth century, perhaps best epitomized by Thomas Mann's *Buddenbrooks*. Like Mann, the Singers focus on the family unit as social microcosm, dramatizing within its parameters the conflicts raging in society at large. Their family sagas follow the conventional path of the social novel, attributing the fall of a prominent house to worldly corruption and subsequent debasement. Chronicling the progressive corrosion of a family over a period of several generations, such novels inevitably depend upon the interpenetration of family and social history. Alike in its broad sweep of space and time, the Jewish family chronicle differs from its European counterpart in the crucial relationship between family and history.

No matter their individual idiosyncrasies, each of Mann's Buddenbrooks is immersed in German history, secure in the knowledge that a new culture, recognizably German, will arise from the ashes of the old. A German, a Frenchman, or an Englishman could change his dress, his religion, his politics without risking linguistic or national disenfranchisement. A European Jew, however, could draw identity only from his religion. Particularly in the East Europe of shifting national boundaries, endemic anti-Semitism, and recurrent pogroms, Jewish history could only tenuously—and ironically—correspond to that of nations in which Jews remained unwelcome aliens. Convinced of their unique destiny as a chosen people, Jews sublimated individual expression to collective aspiration; threatened endlessly by external forces, they relied for survival on internal coherence. While this solidarity could be embodied in the *shtetl* community, it was symbolized most often by the family circle. The disintegration of the Jewish family, therefore, prefigures the destruction of the Jewish people.

Singer announces his theme of dissolution at the outset of *The Family Moskat* in the third marriage of the wealthy eighty-year-old patriarch, Meshulam Moskat. Elsewhere in his fiction Singer treats such marriages and their subsequent fecundity as miraculous guarantors of Jewish survival. But Moskat's "masculine ripple . . . soon flickered and died"; and his bride, the widow Rosa Frumetl Landau, is revealed in their bedchamber "to be a broken shell." Attended by images of sterility, this farcical union defines the essential lifelessness of the Moskat clan. Meshulam's children, themselves already old, lead unproductive lives, powerless to emerge from the long shadow cast by their father. The decay of the Moskat family is palpable in the grotesqueness of Meshulam's four sons: Joel is big-bellied, red-necked, ponderous; Nathan, "a bit lacking in masculinity," has the "high round belly of a pregnant woman"; Pinnie, short and thin, has "a withered, jaundiced face framed in a yellowish-green beard"; and Nyunie is "in a constant lather of quivering, perspiring, flushing."[2] Because Jewish survival is conditioned upon adherence to tradition, and because Judaism is a heavily patriarchal religion, it follows that the rights of the father are uppermost within the Jewish family circle. So long as old Meshulam ruled his house, the Moskat family retained its cohesion. With his death and the inability of his sons to assume his vacated role, the dissolution of the family is foreordained.

THE FAMILY MOSKAT

The aura of death that hovers over *The Family Moskat* is nevertheless only faintly visible in the sterile marriage and failing health of old Meshulam. Its presence is seen increasingly as the organization and setting of the novel snap into focus. Eschewing the classic rise-and-fall pattern of the family chronicle, Singer concentrates exclusively on the Moskats' decline. Abandoning the usual meticulous account of three generations, he portrays a family top-heavy with age, its patriarch dying, its second generation awaiting death. Since the intergenerational conflict so critical to family chronicles has been short-circuited by the inconsequentiality of old Meshulam's children, and since Singer largely disregards the second generation in any case, the pall enveloping the Moskats thickens. Relatively early in the novel Singer shifts his attention away from the Moskat family, locating the classic struggle between religious and secular life styles in a host of characters connected only tangentially with the Moskats. Although Meshulam lingers on for nearly one-third of *The Family Moskat*, by the time he dies he has long outlived his brand of orthodoxy. Many years after his death, Singer invokes his memory in a passage that seals his identification with a dying tradition: "Old Meshulam Moskat had been a king among Jews; and, with all their faults, his sons had managed to stay Jews. But the grandchildren had completely alienated themselves from the old ways. . . . More than twenty years had gone by since old Moskat had died, and the Jewish kingdom over which he had ruled on Gzhybov Place had long been in ruins" (551).

It is the destruction of the "Jewish kingdom," adumbrated in the decline of the Moskat family, that is Singer's true subject. For *The Family Moskat* is ultimately the story of Polish Jewry from the early years of the twentieth century until the Nazi invasion of Poland in 1939. Although every Singer novel with the exception of *Satan in Goray* was written after the Holocaust, *The Family Moskat* is unique in the apocalyptic proximity of its setting. Anticipatory tremors reverberate through such novels as *The Slave,* in which Chmelnicki's barbarities clearly prefigure those of Hitler. But the terminal date of the action of *The Family Moskat* effectively cancels the promise of Jewish communal renewal that exists no matter how tenuously in pre-Holocaust fiction. *The Family Moskat's* leitmotif of death gains its terrible finality from the foreknowledge that European Jewry is doomed. As Singer's Warsaw chronicle draws closer to 1939, the disintegration of Jewish family life simultaneously foreshadows, and is overshadowed by, the impending liquidation of European Jewry. Caught

in the web of history, Singer's Jews are finally powerless to determine their fate: orthodox and enlightened attain an awful equality in the hands of
the Nazi butchers. The curiously flat tone, the series of meaningless relationships, the indirect and
anticlimactic narrative, and the dominant imagery
of death all point to the futility of action. Even in
scenes of high emotion—love affairs, family quarrels, philosophical clashes—the characters sleep-
walk through their parts as if waiting for the end.

Condemned to their 1939 rendezvous with
death, Singer's Warsaw Jews are doubly victims of
history. Soon to be engulfed by the Holocaust,
their fate represents the culmination of a millen-
nium of anti-Semitism. No less are they the unwitting victims of larger forces of European history
that sweep away Gentile and Jew alike. For non-
Jews, Hitler's reign of terror foreclosed an epoch of
European history and altered postwar European
geography. For Jews, it all but ended their history.
This sense of finality, endlessly invoked in post-
Holocaust Jewish literature, is poignantly dramatized by Andre Schwartz-Bart, whose Ernie Levy
(a generic Jewish name) perishes in the Auschwitz
gas chamber in *The Last of the Just* (1960). Because
Levy is the last *Lamed-Vov* (just man), his death not
only signals the end of European Jewry but even
cancels age-old assumptions about human nature.

"At Auschwitz, not only man died but also the idea of man."[3] Where Schwartz-Bart professes to find meaning in Jewish suffering, breathing the sanctity of sacrifice into Levy's death, Singer finds only meaningless pain. At least in *The Family Moskat*, Singer seems to inherit his brother's historical consciousness and the skepticism that it breeds.

Written before the Holocaust, *The Brothers Ashkenazi* expresses the same sense of Jewish futility, even fatality, that pervades *The Family Moskat*. Max Ashkenazi's fierce ambition drives him from *heder* pupil into the maelstrom of the industrial revolution, finally to dominion over the Lodz textile industry. Symbolic of a generation of "enlightened" Jews who shave their beards and modernize their dress in their hunger for worldly success, Max dies as helpless and lonely as any ordinary man: "The gravediggers had already prepared a grave small enough for a child for the King of Lodz. A stranger recited the mourner's prayer. Men stooped to throw handfuls of dirt upon the coffin. 'Dust thou art and unto dust shalt thou return,' they mumbled over their shoulders." *The Brothers Ashkenazi* is a record of its author's disillusionment: initially with the Jews, enlightened and Hasid alike; ultimately with man and the world. Everything comes to nothing, and men—especially Jews—are crushed beneath the brutal juggernaut of history. At Meshulam Moskat's far more sumptuous funeral there is no lack of sons to say Kaddish; yet his financial empire was built upon the same sandy foundation as Ashkenazi's. The deaths of the Jewish "kings" of Lodz and Warsaw symbolize not only the disintegration of their respective communities, but the futility of all worldly aspiration.

In *The Family Moskat*, Singer is constrained either by historical fact or by his brother's example from falling back upon pietistic traditionalism as an antidote to worldly disillusionment. While the very arc of family decline suggests a better past than present or future, and while characters sporadically voice traditional yearnings, the path of repentance is blocked. And even if it weren't, it would lead nowhere. Asa Heshel Bannet embodies the spiritual trauma of the last generation of European Jewry, shoved unwillingly to the foreground of European history, uprooted from their past, adrift in the present, and without a future. A protagonist light years removed from Max Ashkenazi and Meshulam Moskat, those self-fashioned dynamos ruthless in their pursuit of wealth and power, Asa Heshel is no less an end product of historical process. As history lurches toward 1939, Asa Heshel's role is expanded until *The Family Moskat* becomes as much *Bildungsroman* (novel of personal development) as family chronicle; and both record only the tragic second movement in the classic pattern of rise and fall.

From a strictly Jewish perspective Asa Heshel's first appearance is a harbinger of his fate. Fresh from the *shtetl* of Tereshpol Minor and his Talmudic studies, this promising young Hasid materializes one day in Warsaw, having already shaved off his beard and earlocks and discarded his caftan the night before. The "horrifyingly familiar and yet puzzlingly strange" face that confronts him in a mirror is a shocking reminder of his lost identity. Asa Heshel's short journey has spanned two centuries of Jewish history and has taken him from belief to skepticism. The grandson of the saintly Rabbi Dan Katzenellenbogen, whose ancient lineage is rooted in King David and who therein represents Judaism itself, has traded Jewishness for secular humanism, holy scripture for Spinoza. Armed with a worn volume of Spinoza's *Ethics* and bitten by the bug of enlightenment, Asa Heshel first encounters modernity in the person of Abram Shapiro, Meshulam Moskat's son-in-law. An elegantly dressed libertine whose constant philandering is a parody of the personal fulfillment Asa Heshel seeks in Warsaw, Abram betrays his Hasidic roots only by the fur hat he wears on holidays. In Abram's unabashed pursuit of pleasure

Singer indicts the aimless hedonism that characterizes one form of Jewish enlightenment.

Taken by Abram to the house of Nyunie Moskat, Asa Heshel meets in rapid succession each of his future wives—Adele, the emancipated daughter of Rosa Frumetl, and Hadassah, the lovely daughter of Nyunie and Dacha Moskat. Seated at the piano and speaking Polish, Adele is the product of an enlightened Austrian upbringing and a modern secular education. She derides as backward the Warsaw Jews whose gaberdines and skullcaps provoke anti-Semitism; and she answers her mother's shocked rejoinder that her father "also wore a long coat, and sidelocks, too," by proclaiming haughtily that "Papa was a European—a European in every respect" (46). Arguing moreover that Jews and Gentiles coexist "like one family" in her native Austria, Adele exalts a cosmopolitanism that will prove no more satisfactory than Abram's hedonism. Indeed, it is Abram who points out that Polish anti-Semites hate modern Jews more "than the caftaned kind." His reminder that modernity is no refuge for Jews, together with its corollary—that Jew-haters make no distinctions—is one of Singer's, and history's, oft-repeated lessons.

If Adele represents the illusion of assimilation, then Hadassah embodies an even more devastating illusion—that of romantic love. Led into the room by her father, Hadassah "reminded Asa Heshel of the aristocratic young ladies in the romantic novels he had read" (44). A few days later, when she tutors him in Polish, Asa Heshel remarks at her beautiful talk and the poetry in her soul. Still later, when her uncle Moshe Gabriel attributes Hadassah's refusal to marry the pious Fishel Kutner to modern schooling and books "full of adulteries and abominations," the Bialodrevna rabbi, whose own daughter, Gina, proves equally intransigent, replies, "Maybe she's fallen in love—God forbid" (87). Implied in the rabbi's "God forbid" is the traditional Jewish condemnation of romantic love as the basic for marriage. Romantic love strikes at the very heart of Jewish identity—the family—first by denying its primacy, then by denying its purpose. The concept of *mishpoche* (family), with its attendant connotations of kinship and solidarity, dominated *shtetl* society and found its central expression in the relationship between parent and child.[4] In sacrificing parental wishes to rampant individuality, Hadassah reverses the traditional parent-child relationship, and subordinates it to the relationship between lovers. Shifting the chief priority of marriage from childbearing to sensuous fulfillment, romantic lovers undermine the foundation of the Jewish family and jeopardize the survival of Judaism itself.

The many broken marriages of *The Family Moskat* lead to that fragmentation and dispersion of the family which prefigures the destruction of the Jewish community. Because they result most often from mistaken notions of personal fulfillment arising from romantic illusions, these destroyed marriages and the dreary liaisons that replace them constitute a powerful criticism of unchecked individualism. Abram Shapiro, bored with his wife, Hama, drifts through a series of sordid affairs, compulsively unfaithful even to his long-time mistress, Ida Prager. Leah, like Hama a daughter of Meshulam Moskat, runs from her husband, the pious Hasid Moshe Gabriel, to America with Koppel Berman, her late father's unscrupulous overseer. To attain his long-cherished dream of eloping with Leah, Berman cynically abandons his wife and four children. Nyunie Moskat divorces Dacha ("Not a wife—a plague") to become the second husband of the widow Bronya Gritzenhendler, a greater plague. Hadassah, Nyunie's daughter, her love for Asa Heshel frustrated by his marriage to Adele, reluctantly marries Fishel Kutner, only to desert him when Asa Heshel again becomes available. Asa Heshel, whose sudden marriage to Adele is one of the most conspicuous of the many mismatchings of *The Family Moskat*, leaves her to live with, and eventually to marry, Hadassah. Finally he takes up with the revolutionary convert, Barbara Fishelsohn, having long since disclaimed all but the most perfunctory responsibility for his son and daughter by Adele and Hadassah respectively. Because no love relationship endures, and new liaisons are no more rewarding than old, marriage in *The Family Moskat* becomes an inverted metaphor for the dissolution of the family and of Jewish tradition, rather than for their perpetuation.

If the discordant or shattered family is the institutional locus of fraying Jewish tradition, then Asa Heshel Bannet is its individual embodiment. One of Singer's most perplexed and perplexing characters, Asa Heshel is the first of his novelistic self-portraits. Endlessly poring over the very volume of Spinoza that first shook Singer's faith, Asa Heshel incorporates the traditional background and the modern rootlessness of his creator. Like Singer, he leapfrogs the centuries from *shtetl* to city, in the process becoming the stereotypical modern Jew: urban, restless, alienated. As he futilely seeks happiness apart from God and community, he comes to epitomize the spiritual malaise of the modern Jew. At their last meeting

THE FAMILY MOSKAT

Asa Heshel confesses his physical and spiritual sickness to Adele, who advises him to consult a psychiatrist. "Then," replies Asa Heshel, "every Jew in the world would have to go to one. I mean every modern Jew." All but a few of Singer's Warsaw Jews suffer an identity crisis symbolized by the distorted mirror images that confront such apostates as Asa Heshel, Hadassah, Abram Shapiro, and Koppel Berman at critical points in *The Family Moskat*. Lost or confused identity is best dramatized late in the novel at the Channukah masquerade ball where Asa Heshel first meets Barbara Fishelsohn. Jews dressed in a bewildering variety of costumes swirl madly together in an obscene parody of Hasidic ecstasy. Among the masked figures—Russian generals, Polish grandees, spike-helmeted Germans—drift "rabbis in fur hats, yeshivah students in velvet skullcaps, sidelocks dangling below their ears." Traditional dress, once the visible mark of Jewish identity, has shrunk to the status of ball costume. "What the devil are they carrying on for, these exiled vagabonds," muses Asa Heshel. "They had lost God and had not won the world" (491).

Passing judgment on his fellow Jews, Asa Heshel judges himself. As Singer's first modern protagonist and the prototype of his later fictional heroes, Asa Heshel flails about in a futile search for happiness without God. Among those secular panaceas beckoning to newly emancipated Jews, Communism and Zionism are the most alluring. Drawn to Communism, Asa Heshel is put off first by its scapegoating, then by its brutality. Likening the Communist strategy of blaming social ills on the capitalists to the anti-Semite blaming Jews, Asa Heshel imagines endless recrimination displacing the Communist ideal of universal brotherhood. Echoing the disillusioned Jewish trade unionists of *The Brothers Ashkenazi* who found that their Gentile co-workers regarded them primarily as Jews, only secondarily as comrades, Singer implies that man's eternal need for scapegoats overrides his more humane instincts. But it is his witnessing of the bloodbath unleashed by the Bolsheviks in the wake of the 1917 Russian Revolution that so sickens Asa Heshel as to end his brief flirtation with Communism. Rivaling the czars in their ferocity, the new masters of Russia convince Asa Heshel that their brave new world is little better than the old. So profound is his disillusionment that he amazes Barbara by stating his preference for capitalism: "It's very cruel, but it's human nature and the economic law" (495).

While Zionism fares better than Communism in *The Family Moskat*, it too is ultimately rejected by Asa Heshel. Beset alike by the usual anti-Semitism of Polish nationalists and the unforeseen anti-Semitism of Bolsheviks, both ominously counterpointed by Hitler's rise in Germany, many Jews of Asa Heshel's generation saw no future for themselves in Europe. After his first brush with anti-Semitism on the streets of Warsaw, Asa Heshel recalls Abram's warning that modern Jews fare no better than the orthodox and determines to flee Poland. Convinced by the Zionists that Jews must establish their own nation, Asa Heshel remains nonetheless in Warsaw, prey to his own mounting lack of faith in all collective solutions. The closer he draws to Zionism, the keener he imagines its internal divisions and external oppositions. Yet Asa Heshel's disavowal of Zionism springs less from its perceived weaknesses than from Rabbi Katzenellenbogen's reservations. When Asa Heshel tells his grandfather of the Zionist dream of a Jewish state, the old rabbi maintains that a Jewish homeland makes sense only for believers: "If, he insisted, they had no further belief in the Bible, then why should they have any longing for the Biblical land of the Jews" (238). Rabbi Dan's words effectively conflate Zionism with Communism as secular versions of false messianism.

Unable to regain his lost Jewishness and unconvinced by Communists and Zionists, Asa Heshel is progressively driven back upon his own

resources. Yet personal life proves no more rewarding than communal life. "The Laboratory of Happiness," his unfinished thesis, is a maze of endless
contradictions testifying to the failure of his scholarly ambitions and of his hedonistic philosophy.
Seeking fulfillment in love, Asa Heshel proves
ironically unable to love. His marriages to Adele
and Hadassah and his affair with Barbara add up
to little more than recurrent episodes of sexual ex-
ploitation. Domestic routine bores him and is increasingly punctuated by long separations from his
wives. Wanting no children, Asa Heshel neglects
those he accidentally fathers and bases his "philosophy" on a strict regimen of birth control: "More
sex and fewer children." Sex, as an end in itself
rather than a means of procreation and continuity,
is inevitably coupled with death in *The Family
Moskat*. Its invalidity as a life principle is signaled
by Asa Heshel's growing cynicism, best expressed
in his silence following Adele's "Tell me truthfully,
were you ever in love with anyone?" The endlessly
aborted chapters of "The Laboratory of Happiness" reflect Asa Heshel's lost sense of purpose;
he finally crams the pages of the ironically titled
manuscript into a stove. Adele's last thoughts
about Asa Heshel might serve equally as an epitaph for "emancipated" Jewry: "He was one of
those who must serve God or die. He had for-

saken God, and because of this he was dead—a living body with a dead soul" (581–82).

Near the end of part 9 the many spiritual deaths of *The Family Moskat* exfoliate into a vision of general doom. At the bedside of the dying Abram, Asa Heshel extrapolates, from the fragmentation of the Jewish community and the rise of Hitler, the coming Holocaust: "They'll destroy all of us. . . . The end of our world *has* come" (535). Fittingly, the novel's tenth, and final, part opens with an account of the widely expanded Moskat Moskat cemetery plot where Abram has now joined old Meshulam and the greater part of the Moskat clan. Singer juxtaposes the many Moskat graves and the scattering of the remaining Hasidim with Hitler's growing menace and the imminence of war to fill his concluding pages with the imagery of dissolution and death. The effect is subtly to magnify the calculus of impotence expressed earlier by the enlightened Hertz Yanovar when he is hauled in for questioning by the Polish police: "We are powerless not only in relation to the Christians, but to our own brethren as well" (518). Caught up in the tide of history all Jews, enlightened and orthodox alike, are equally powerless. When Asa Heshel thrusts "The Laboratory of Happiness" into the stove a few days after the outbreak of World War II, he reenacts the identical gesture of his grandfather, Rabbi Dan, who burned three sackfuls of his own manuscripts shortly after the outbreak of World War I. Consigning the fruits of a lifetime of wrestling with ultimate problems to the flames, both apostate and saint testify to the failure of their world views.

Singer's historical hindsight forces *The Family Moskat* into a pattern more characteristic of *The Brothers Ashkenazi* than of his own fiction. Max Ashkenazi scribbles as feverishly as Asa Heshel or Rabbi Dan; like theirs, his calculations come to nothing in the face of the overwhelming conclusion of *The Brothers Ashkenazi*: that finally all Jews "are puny and helpless before the large brutal forces of the external world."[5] Running into Hertz Yanovar in a Warsaw street reduced to rubble by German bombs, Asa Heshel is informed, "The Messiah will come soon." To the incredulous Asa Heshel, Hertz goes on the explain, "Death is the Messiah. That's the real truth" (611). Years earlier, suffering from hunger, cold, and sickness during a bitter Warsaw winter, and plagued by an inner voice that urged him to put an end to it all, the young Singer arrived at an identical conclusion: "There is but one redemption and that is death."[6]

Singer's nihilism, equally the product of historical inevitability and of his own fitful despair, casts the deeper pall of hopelessness over the final

THE FAMILY MOSKAT

movement of *The Family Moskat*. Hertz's last words
recall the fate of Hadassah, killed by a German
bomb; of Adele, thrown back from Palestine "like
garbage"; of Asa Heshel and of Hertz himself, fro-
zen by their despair in devastated Warsaw; and ultimately of European Jewry. In the Yiddish version
of *The Family Moskat,* however, a final chapter celebrates Jewish piety and holds out the possibility of
spiritual redemption. Asa Heshel and other similarly enlightened Jews see the error of their ways
and, born again, return to the fold of traditional
Judaism. The nihilism of Asa Heshel's parting
words to Barbara—"I want to die"—offered up to
explain his refusal to join her in fleeing doomed
Warsaw, is converted by the Yiddish ending into
something like affirmation. Thus the very fact that
he chooses to stay behind with his fellow Jews constitutes his belated acceptance of the communal
ties that bind. Such didacticism is endemic in Yiddish literature and common to Singer's endings.
But in *The Family Moskat*, Singer has orchestrated a
symphony of death so massive as to resist a senti-
mental finale. Precisely because the novel invokes
a historical reality too powerful and too horrible to
dismiss or even to mediate, its English ending is
compelling. Even if Asa Heshel wished symbolically to retrace his steps from modern city back to
medieval *shtetl*, his path would be blocked by Hit-

ler, whose war against the Jews renders piety and apostasy equally irrelevant. Onto the lesson that you can't go home again, Singer has grafted the historical fact that no home remains, in order to produce in the English translation of *The Family Moskat* perhaps his most "modern" novel.

The Manor and *The Estate*

The German bombs that reduce Warsaw to rubble and foreshadow the Holocaust invoke the apocalyptic vision of historical closure. It is the harrowing possibility that Hitler will write *finis* to Jewish as well as to Polish history that haunts the last chapters of *The Family Moskat*. Sharing the premonitory tremors of *The Family Moskat* but not its historical proximity to the Holocaust, *The Manor* and *The Estate* resist the nearly inevitable nihilism of their predecessor. History, which forecloses moral choice in *The Family Moskat*, renders it imperative in *The Manor* and *The Estate*. *The Manor* opens in 1863, the year of the unsuccessful Polish insurrection against Russian rule, when Jews began trading the traditional passivity of ghetto life for more active and prominent roles on the national stage. "All the spiritual and intellectual ideas that triumphed in the modern era had their roots in the world of that time—socialism and nationalism, Zionism and assimilationism, nihilism and anarchism, suffragettism, atheism, the weakening of the family bond, free love, and even the beginnings of Fascism," maintains Singer in his note to the original edition of *The Manor.*[7] It is the world portrayed by I. J. Singer in *The Brothers Ashkenazi:* "Lodz seethed in ferment as the city grew day by day, home by home." Caught up in the quickening rhythm of Poland's belated industrial revolution, Jews deserted their dreary *shtetls* for the equally dreary urban ghettos of Lodz and Warsaw. Calman Jacoby, the paterfamilias of *The Manor,* all but completes his swift metamorphosis from tradesman to tycoon by the end of chapter 1. The rise of Jacoby (whose name, like Ashkenazi, refers to the Jewish people) leads to the prosperity of other Jews who follow him out of The Sands, on the outskirts of Jampol, into the town proper—hitherto prohibited to Jews. And in Warsaw, so changed since the aborted rebellion that Calman barely recognizes it, Jewish residents crowd once-forbidden streets.

Yet the new social dynamics that enable Jews to prosper contain the seeds of their undoing. To oversee his extensive property on horseback, Calman discards the ankle-length caftan of the pious Jew for a short coat. Because he "had to assert himself everywhere" to prevent bandits from stealing his timber, Calman endlessly patrols his newly acquired forest, leading two dogs and carrying a gun. Exhausted by business concerns, he is hard pressed to retain his piety, only compensating for his forgotten twilight prayers by repeating the Eighteen Benedictions during his evening devotions. Soon he comes to understand the meaning of the Talmudic saying: "The more property, the more anxiety." Vowing to curtail his burgeoning enterprises, Calman finds that success generates its own momentum. Having to supply railroad ties for the czar, he is forced to employ Russian-speaking Lithuanian Jews whose beardless faces and Gentile clothes smack of heresy. To fuel his many enterprises he borrows money from Wallenberg, a rich Warsaw financier and a convert to Catholicism. Such outward marks of success as fancy clothes and a refurbished house—like the dogs and gun, the enlightened Lithuanians, and the apostate Wallenberg—draw Calman closer to Gentile worldliness and further from Jewish spirituality. Only on the Sabbath is he able to find respite from the press of worldly affairs and thereby momentarily to arrest his spiritual decline.

The conjunction of material wealth and spiritual impoverishment in Calman Jacoby suggests the danger of worldly ambition. Prosperity not only threatens Calman's spiritual well-being but unleashes the disruptive forces that undermine Jewish family life and Judaism itself. The exact nature of such forces and the responses they typically elicit are dramatized in the marriage of Calman's four daughters. Jochebed, the eldest, dutiful and shy, marries the conventional and traditional Mayer Joel and settles down to a placid life reminiscent of her mother's; Shaindel, lively and coquettish, marries the son of a Hasidic rabbi, Ezriel Babad, who eventually metamorphoses into an enlightened intellectual and scientist. It is in the marriages of Calman's two younger daughters, however, that Singer evokes the starkest polarities of Jewish experience. Miriam Lieba, her dreams filled with the stuff of romantic novels, elopes with Count Lucian Jampolski, a rabid anti-Semite whose murderous career epitomizes the depraved Polish nobility. Tsipele, the youngest, pious and obedient, marries Jochanen, destined to become the rabbi of the Marshinov Hasidim. Lucian and Jochanen—devil and saint—represent the extremes of Jewish alienation and integration. Seduced by illusions of romantic love, Miriam Lieba refuses her father's choice—Jochanen—for Lucian, abandoning her family and her religion in the process. With Lucian she flies to Paris, where her dreams of luxury find ironic resolution in a life so miserable that she must take in laundry to keep from starving. Tsipele's is the female role extolled by Jewish tradition: dutiful, fruitful, subservient, basking in the glow of her husband's legendary piety. In the outward uneventfulness of her life lies its greatest achievement. Significantly it is Miriam Lieba, the only Jacoby daughter to refuse an arranged marriage, who ends disastrously. And it is Calman himself who engineers his daughter's fall by allowing her to choose her husband in the first place.

In part 1 of *The Manor* the rising arc of Calman's worldliness creates the context for Miriam Lieba's downfall. Aware of the romantic egoism that led to her undoing, Calman nonetheless comes dangerously close to reenacting her apostasy in part 2. Here the focus shifts from the effect of his worldliness upon his family to its growing effect upon himself. With the breakup of his family resulting from his daughters' marriages and his wife's death, Calman falls prey to loneliness and to the desire for a son to perpetuate his name. But his ensuing marriage to the sensuous and sophisticated Clara Kaminer, a widow half his age, is motivated chiefly by the unquenchable lust that marks his spiritual dereliction. One of Singer's classic mismatchings, the marriage soon turns into a parody of Jewish family life, characterized by Clara's unfaithfulness, Calman's depression, and the brutish nature of their son, Sasha. Likened to Lucian in his perversity, the all but Gentile Sasha is a living symbol of Calman's folly and a reminder of Miriam Lieba's. When Calman and Clara take up residence in the former Jampolski manor, the identification between the rising Jewish and the falling Polish aristocracy is nearly complete.

To win the manor is to win its metaphorical equivalent—the world. Calman's is an empty victory, its spuriousness crystallized in a party scene reminiscent of the costume ball in *The Family Moskat*. Again the party's sophisticated veneer masks its underlying superficiality and licentiousness. And again a mirror is the instrument of self-revelation. Catching a glimpse of himself in his fashionable knee-length frock coat, Calman imagines his beard equally shortened. Reflexively blaming Clara for trimming his beard—and for tempting him toward the apostasy a shortened beard represents—Calman ends by cursing himself. For Calman it is the moment of epiphany. By the end of part 2 of *The Manor* he has decided to divorce Clara, to transfer his business enterprises to Mayer Joel, and to embrace "the life of a Jew."

Calman's return to Jewishness is realized in the two symbolic journeys he undertakes in part 3. The first takes him to Jochanen's court at Marshinov in time for Rosh Hashanah, the Jewish

New Year, the beginning of the holy period culminating in Yom Kippur, the Day of Atonement. By timing Calman's arrival in Marshinov to coincide with the holiest of Jewish holidays and their ancient promise of spiritual renewal, Singer shapes the journey into a powerful reaffirmation of faith. Calman's second journey is shorter—from the manor back to the same house he had lived in with his first wife—but no less profound. Living in one room, sustained by the black bread and water that nourished him in former days, Calman ministers to passersby and prays in a makeshift synagogue. There, protected by shelves of sacred books whose "letters were steeped in holiness, in eternity," Calman feels united with the patriarchs, "a partner in sharing the Torah's treasures" (442). Calman's journey of the prodigal son, which has taken him into the world and onto the brink of apostasy, ends in contemplation of the holy letters that dissolve the world and immerse him in the timeless stream of Jewish history.

Singer's dim view of human history is reflected in the tripartite structure of his penitential novels. Only by rejecting the world does his Jewish Everyman complete a spiritual voyage of discovery that leads him from orthodoxy through waywardness back to orthodoxy. Calman Jacoby's errors derived from sensual and material temptations. Never did this essentially simple man lose his orthodox Jewish belief amidst the welter of competing ideologies listed in Singer's preface. Because he never ceased to believe in the value system of traditional Judaism, his redemptive journey is relatively straightforward and unambiguous. While *The Estate* recapitulates the tripartite organization, the symbolic design, and the spiritual journey of *The Manor*, its hero, Ezriel Babad, is a man very different from his father-in-law. Son of a Hasidic rabbi, Babad is, like Asa Heshel Bannet, a Singer self-portrait, whose attraction to modernity, unlike Calman's, stems from intellectual pride and ambition. *The Estate*, therefore, plays out its author's habitual drama of deviance and penitence on a historical and moral field roughly equidistant from those of *The Manor* and *The Family Moskat*.

Ezriel Babad is Singer's portrait of the humanist as scientist. Convinced that science points the way to human betterment and increasingly unable to accept religious revelation or dogma, Ezriel nevertheless believes, "Man must continuously seek God." His search takes the form of associating God with medicine and dissociating Him from traditional Judaism. Ezriel's is a brand of false messianism ultimately as ruinous as the Communism of his sister, Mirale: "Now he spent his time cutting the dead apart, and Mirale plotted to kill the living" (330). Long before his conflation of the living with the dead, while still nominally a Hasid, Ezriel had previewed the direction his life would take during a stay with Calman in Marshinov. There the Hasidic joy that moves his father-in-law leaves him cold. Already the rationalist, Ezriel seeks truth only in "the things that can be weighed and measured." His confusion, symbolized by his inability to locate his lodgings, provokes Singer's cryptic "Ezriel has lost his way." Before he can acknowledge his error, much less find his way back to the spiritual values thus casually jettisoned in his youth, Ezriel will have to pass through Singer's familiar cycle of worldliness and disillusionment to repentance.

Although Ezriel's inner struggle has little in common with Calman's, their outward waywardness finds similar expression in the sort of material and sexual "success" that soon turns rancid. The growth of Ezriel's medical practice coincides with his growing attraction to Olga Bielikov, a "modern" woman as different from his first wife as Clara was from Shaindel's mother. Herself permanently estranged from Judaism, Olga is revolted by "primitive" Jewish dress and customs. Topolka, her country estate, is purchased with funds bequeathed her by the convert Wallenberg, whose previous financial dealings with Calman and Ezriel implied the cost of worldly success. Olga's acquisition of the estate is the moral equivalent of Calman's takeover of the Jampolski manor. Formerly owned by dissolute Polish aristocrats, both properties serve as metaphors for a fallen world in which Jews become the inheritors of Gentile corruption. Topolka is the appropriate scene for yet another dress ball, a favorite Singer microcosm of the world at large. It falls on the eve of the Ninth of Ab, a date sacred to Jewish memory, when, after a last meal of bread, ashes, and a hard-boiled egg, orthodox Jews fast in commemoration of the tragedy of the destruction of the temple of Jerusalem. At Topolka, however, great numbers of ducks and geese are slaughtered to provide a lavish banquet for a mixed assemblage of Jewish and Gentile revelers. A pig, roasting on a spit, is an especially jarring symbol of the desecration of a holy day and of the implicit identification of Jews with Gentiles. Moreover, it is also at the ball that Olga's daughter, Natasha, meets Fyodor, the romantic lieutenant with whom she later elopes. The calamitous results of this liaison recall the fate Miriam Lieba suffered with Lucian, and lead to Olga's eventual breakdown. While it is true that Natasha's elopement sows the seeds of Olga's destruction and of the disintegration of Ezriel's second household, it is important to remember that Olga herself culti-

vated the seedbed: the party at Topolka sealed her
daughter's tragedy and her own.

Abandoned soon after the ball, Topolka becomes a fast-decaying monument to the futility of
worldliness: "Landowning was not for Jews," concludes Ezriel. The proper use of worldly goods
is illustrated by Tsipele, who sells her earrings to
pay for Shaindel's burial, and by Jochanen, who
presses his gold watch upon a poor man to pay for
medical advice about his daughter's illness. Still,
Ezriel's attraction to enlightenment takes the primary form not of material, but of intellectual ambition. Seeing enlightened Jews governed by the
same irrationality that repelled him in the orthodox, Ezriel is nonetheless too much the rationalist
to deny the power of reason itself. In his career as
neurologist and psychiatrist Ezriel may resemble
Freud, whose theories Singer reflexively distrusts.
Like those who worship Mammon or Marx, Freud-
ians are cosmopolitan in their assumptions about
universal human drives. It is this cosmopolitanism
that breaks down the distinctions between Jew and
Gentile, that denies the uniqueness of the Jewish
experience, and that inevitably betrays Singer's
emancipated Jews who envision a utopia of equal
coexistence with Poles or Russians or Germans.
Fitful but increasingly frequent outbursts of anti-
Semitism in *The Estate* convince Ezriel of the limi-

tations of reason. Singer juxtaposes Ezriel's prescription of hydrotherapy for an impotent bridegroom with Jochanen's promise to the recipient of his gold watch of his daughter's recovery. Jochanen's blind faith is manifestly no more irrational than Ezriel's hydrotherapy, itself perhaps a "scientific" parody of the Jewish ritual bath.

Unlike Freud, Ezriel believes in God. Like Freud, however, he believes that a Jew can remain a Jew outside the network of traditional Jewish relationships. For Singer this "rational" response to the pressures of modernity is profoundly irrational, merely stripping the enlightened Jew of the communal bonding which, no matter how fragile, defines his Jewishness in the first place. Alexander Zipkin—a mindless "intellectual," grab bag of fashionable opinions, and Clara's seducer—represents enlightenment run amok. Spouting Darwin and Marx, Zipkin argues that man is "just another animal," and that the Polish Jew, unproductive, ignorant of the language of the country in which he lived, and mired in outworn customs, is "little more than a parasite." Neither Zipkin nor Mirale, Ezriel's sister and an apostle of violent revolution who similarly castigates Jewish backwardness, seems to fathom the anti-Semitism latent in their "progressivism." Both unwittingly invoke the scapegoat role forced upon the Jews by anti-

Semites; and both implicitly condone the actions of their persecutors. That Zipkin eventually becomes a doctor constitutes Singer's ironic commentary on secular humanism.

Although Ezriel is never seduced by the politics of revolutionary violence, he falls prey to its complementary modern ideology: romantic love. As usual Singer couples lust and violence in his indictment of modern European culture. Violence—theoretical in Zipkin, frighteningly real in the murderous Lucian—underlies their respective liaisons with Clara and Miriam Lieba. Both relationships are attended by images of death and dissolution. Clara, like Lucian, is so obsessed with death that she likens the bed in which she and Zipkin first make love to a cemetery. And the marriage bed she shares with Calman engenders Sasha, whose volatile mix of lust and violence comes to rival Lucian's. While the link between lust and violence is not so firmly established at its onset, Ezriel comes eventually to recognize his affair with Olga as a form of sexual violence. Like Clara and Miriam Lieba, Olga devours romantic novels. All three reenact romantic narratives with disastrous results consequent upon their religious apostasy. Flying from the strictures of Jewish orthodoxy, they are undone by the false freedom of modernity. Olga, modern woman and convert, forever sneering at Jewish backwardness, is a devotee of spiritualism, a pale and pathetic stand-in for religious belief. Her spiritualism, no less than Zipkin's Darwinism, Mirale's Marxism, and Ezriel's Freudianism, represents the failed challenge posed by modernity to tradition.

With Ezriel's growing awareness of the failures of modernism comes a corresponding sense of his own shortcomings. So long as he is unable to diagnose the essential lawlessness of modern life styles, Ezriel can attribute sick personal relationships—including his own with Olga—to individual weaknesses. As a psychiatrist he believes that the problems of modern life are capable of rational solutions, never imagining that such problems are engendered by modernity itself and are therefore insoluble by modern means. To drive this lesson home Singer recapitulates Mirale's story in that of Zina, who, like her aunt, is an apostle of violent revolution. Ezriel's discovery of his daughter's gun constitutes a spiritual epiphany: "The children testified to the hypocrisy of their fathers" (675). In his vain pursuit of personal fulfillment as in his failure to educate his children as Jews, he has translated the dream of freedom from the strictures of the Jewish God into the nightmare of enslavement to false idols. Himself imprisoned by lust, he has created the conditions of Zina's incar-

ceration for revolutionary conspiracy. Zina's gun—
the first such "instrument of destruction" he had
ever touched—"astounded" Ezriel by its weight. It
is a symbol of the world of Gentile violence to
which Ezriel's benign modern neglect has exposed
his daughter, and a heavy reminder of the ancient
dictum that a father's sins are visited upon his
children.

Singer's close juxtaposition of Zina's gun and
the Topolka ball offers the most powerful of his
many proofs that Jewish life is meaningless apart
from Judaism. Only Dr. Marion Zawacki—a
Gentile—is able to live the life of service and un-
compromising rectitude based on rational principles that Ezriel had reserved for himself. And it
is ironic that Ezriel's recantation—"I am no
rationalist"—is delivered to Zawacki's widow. In
his disclaimer and its echo—"What is called nerves
is a moral illness" (784)—lies Ezriel's admission of
personal and professional failure. From such ac-
knowledgments stem contrition and repentance,
the necessary preliminaries to redemption. As
usual, Singer's penitent must translate abstract desire into moral action. For Ezriel, no less than it did
for Calman, this involves a journey to Marshinov,
the symbolic antithesis of the manor and the estate. That Ezriel is motivated not merely by secular
disenchantment, but by the positive moral com-

mitment that fuels his desire to break with Olga and to leave their son Moishe with Tsipele to be raised as a Jew, expands the journey's symbolic dimensions. In Marshinov, Ezriel finds joy in the Hasidism he had once reviled, but remains powerless to surrender his "reason." Jochanen, understanding that his brother-in-law can draw no closer to belief, accepts the combination of Ezriel's change of heart and his salvation of Moishe as the moral equivalent of faith.

Lacking the faith that inspires Jochanen and that motivated Calman's retirement to the synagogue, Ezriel can hardly embrace the traditional way of life theoretically demanded of Singer's penitents. And even if he could, the Marshinov way of life has fallen victim to history. Jochanen's death prefigures Marshinov's decline; his son Zadok, who might have succeeded him, is, like the young Ezriel, a believer in enlightenment. Barred psychologically and historically from doing penance by traditional means, Ezriel grasps at the only remaining alternative: Zionism. His letter to Zadok, written from Switzerland en route to Palestine, contains his (and Singer's) bitter denunciation of Europe and justification of Zionism. Writing less than a decade after the Holocaust destroyed European Jewry, Singer is forced to modify the orthodox view of Zionism as merely a seductive brand of assimilation. That Palestine represents for Ezriel's generation what Marshinov represented for Calman's is the retrospective legacy of history. Hindsight adds urgency to Ezriel's penitential journey, for Palestine symbolizes not only spiritual renewal for one Jew but survival for the Jewish people.

The personal sagas of Singer's three Jewish Everymen rise like bas-reliefs from the massive architecture of his family chronicles. Asa Heshel Bannet, Calman Jacoby, and Ezriel Babad are products of the many historical forces that threaten traditional Jewish life both from within and without. Because history for Singer takes the form, not of progression, but of eternal recurrence, it offers no hope to his expectant Jews. Only in the otherworldly timelessness of their own history can Jews find refuge from their persecutors. Writing to Zadok from Bern, Ezriel confesses his suicidal thoughts and how they were dispelled by his joy in seeing "real Jews" in Hasidic study houses. Such Jews, who "do not even know that we are at the end of the 'magnificent' and bloody nineteenth century" (808), are the "true realists," for they have freed themselves from the perpetual flux of human history. Although he cannot follow them into the study house, Ezriel sees in the pious Hasidim the powerful reflection of his own Jewish-

ness, which he affirms in words hauntingly evo-
cative of Freud's: "I can deny God, but I cannot
stop being a Jew."[8] At the epiphanic moment
that reveals the inalterable tragedy of the historical role they were born to play, Singer's protagonists turn from the folly of worldly striving
toward the different geography of their final
destinations—the synagogue for Calman, Palestine
for Ezriel, bombed-out Warsaw for Asa Heshel. No
matter the byways they follow, their paths lead to
the same truth: that Judaism confers their only
identity.

Notes

1. Irving H. Buchen, *Isaac Bashevis Singer and the Eternal Past* (New
York: New York University Press, 1968) 22.

2. Isaac Bashevis Singer, *The Family Moskat* (New York: Noonday
Press, 1950) 66–67. Page references given in parentheses refer to this
edition.

3. Elie Wiesel, *Legends of Our Time* (New York: Holt Rinehart,
1968) 190.

4. Sol Gittleman, *From Shtetl to Suburbia* (Boston: Beacon Press,
1978) 2, 86.

5. Irving Howe, introduction, I. J. Singer, *The Brothers Ashkenazi*
(New York: Bantam, 1980) xv.

6. Singer, *Love and Exile* (Garden City, NY: Doubleday, 1984) 51.

7. "*The Manor* and *The Estate* were written as one book . . . and I
am happy that they are now coming out in one volume under the title

of the first part," explains Singer in a note to the 1979 edition (New York: Farrar, Straus). Page references are to this edition.

8. See, e.g., the 1930 preface to the Hebrew translation of *Totem and Taboo*. Freud describes himself as one "who is completely estranged from the religion of his fathers . . . but who has yet never repudiated his people, who feels that he is in his essential nature a Jew and who has no desire to alter that nature."

CHAPTER FOUR

The Magician of Lublin and *The Penitent*

The penitential action that so often inspires the final movement of a Singer novel finds its most urgent and radical expression in *The Magician of Lublin* and *The Penitent*. Because Yasha Mazur and Joseph Shapiro stray so far from the Jewish community, their return can be effected only be spectacularly wrenching acts of penance. So frayed is their Jewishness that they must struggle to regain the very idea of community; and only by means of sharply restricted definitions of community can they inoculate themselves against the bacillus of worldliness. As if to acknowledge the fragility of their recovered identity as Jews, they ratify it by returning across the entire spectrum of Jewish life to the orthodoxy of beards, sidelocks, and ritual garments. Traditional appearance and dress become the visible guarantors of the narrowly constricted life styles they obsessively seek. Whether bricked in (Mazur) or transplanted (Shapiro), the two penitents understand that only by virtual imprisonment can the stability of their new identities be ensured.

The Magician of Lublin

The Magician of Lublin, serialized in the *Forward* in 1959 and published the following year in English, is the first of Singer's novels to skip the intermediary stage of Yiddish publication in book form, thereby setting the pattern for all his future novels. It is a watershed novel in the far more important sense of signaling a change in authorial direction. From the destiny of the Jewish people as reflected in the complicated groupings of his family chronicles, Singer turns to the fate of the individual. Not that the personal idiosyncrasies of an Asa Heshel Bannet or an Ezriel Babad went unnoticed; rather they were subsumed into phases of Jewish history which were themselves shaped by larger historical forces. Beginning with *The Magician of Lublin,* Singer's protagonists are motivated far less by historical necessity than by psychological propensity. The psychological transformation that launches Yasha Mazur on Singer's characteristic journey of the prodigal son takes place within a structure that combines aspects of the picaresque (travel) novel and the *Kunstleroman* (artist novel). In Singer's treatment, however, the wanderings that normally open onto bright new vistas only lead his *picaro* to a dead end; and the deepening self-awareness of the nature of art which conventionally preludes creative maturity only leads his *Kunstler* to renunciation.

As a magician Yasha earns his living by endlessly crisscrossing Poland, returning to his home base in Lublin and to his faithful wife, Esther, only between engagements. Famous throughout Poland as the Magician of Lublin, he is merely notorious in Lublin, which at the end of the nineteenth century remains the seat of a stable and long-established Jewish community. Yasha is personable and generous, but impious, appearing in the synagogue only on Rosh Hashanah and Yom Kippur, and then only to pacify Esther. Clean-shaven and acrobatically supple, looking far younger than his forty years, he is the antithesis of the gray-bearded and prematurely aged Jews of Lublin. Yasha's freedom contrasts sharply with the stasis of traditional communal life, but it is expressed chiefly in the countless extramarital affairs which reduce his freedom to license. Based upon the premise that monogamy results in melancholy, his constant philandering is itself the result of boredom and depression. Yasha is like one of those characters from the pages of Knut Hamsun, who, claims Singer in his 1967 preface to *Hunger*, "was perhaps the first to show how childish the so-called grownups are. His heroes are all children—as romantic as children, as irrational, and often as savage. Hamsun discovered even before Freud did that love and sex are a child's game." Boyishly greedy for experience, Yasha is forever in the act of becoming, his oddly unfinished status reflected in his ever-changing sexual partners and travel destinations.

Yasha's archetypal odyssey from stable Lublin to tumultuous Warsaw and back initially takes the form of successive visits to his various women. His first stop—to pick up Magda, his Gentile assistant and mistress, who loves him with doglike devotion—turns into a parody of home life with Esther in Lublin. And the sinister presence of Magda's cut-throat brother, Bolek, completes the habitual Singer equation of lust with violence. In the nearby town of Piask, Yasha drops in on Zeftel, the deserted wife of one of the Jewish thieves, and reminds her to look him up in Warsaw. That Yasha, fresh from Magda's bed and looking forward to seeing his "true" love Emilia in Warsaw, entangles himself still further with Zeftel is the result of a

boredom which transcends lust. Emilia, respect-
able middle-class widow of a Polish professor,
refuses to yield before marriage, and insists that
Yasha divorce his wife and convert to Catholicism.
At the same time that he professes undying love
for Emilia, Yasha wonders whether his attraction
to Halina, her adolescent daughter, isn't even
stronger. In his various incarnations—as eternal
bridegroom to the seldom-seen Esther; as lover-
father to the slight and youthful Magda; as lover-
son to the broad-hipped and full-bosomed Zeftel;
as gentleman suitor to the genteel and proper
Emilia; and as father-protector to the romantic and
worshipful Halina—he resists final definition. Jug-
gling the sexual, social, and religious possibilities
epitomized by these women, Yasha remains forever young and unfinished.

Although his compulsive role-playing goes far
beyond the theatricality demanded by his profession, Yasha's self-fashioning is analogous to his
magical illusions. After astounding the thieves of
Piask with his lock-picking skill, he wonders how
he, the lover of Emilia, can consort with such low-
lifes: "But that's how he was," Yasha concludes.
"There was always another role for him to play.
He was a maze of personalities—religious and
heretical, good and evil, false and sincere."[1] Emilia,
Magda, Zeftel, and the Piask thieves are all locks

waiting to be picked by Yasha, the master lock-smith. Just as lock-picking—and hypnosis—symbolize his art, another tool of the magician's trade—the tightrope—provides the image of his precarious existence. Although admirers refer constantly to Yasha as an artist rather than a magician, the terms are ultimately interchangeable. Even a magic which attains the status of art consists mainly in subverting nature; it becomes a metaphor for the same draining away of meaning by which Yasha destabilizes his identity. Yasha, like the heroes of the Hamsun novels which influenced Singer, is "nothing but a chaos of moods that kept constantly changing, often without a trace of consistency" (*Hunger,* xii). Such inconsistency, no matter how common in modern man, denotes waywardness in Singer's Jews.

Jewish identity derives from God's covenant with His chosen people. A Jew is one who not only believes in the Jewish God and His commandments but who shares a Jewish corporate identity. With the rise of European nation-states Jewish identity, already eroded by enlightenment secularism, met its greatest challenge, summarized in Clermont-Tonnerre's famous formula: "To the Jews as a nation—nothing; to them as individuals—everything."[2] Willing to grant them political rights but unwilling to tolerate their "nation within a na-

tion," the French revolutionists presented the Jews
with a hard choice. Either dilute Jewish identity, by
agreeing that Jewishness consists only of a set of
commonly held religious beliefs, or remain permanently outside the society at large. Seduced by the
promise of civic equality, masses of West European
Jews traded their corporate identity for various degrees of social assimilation. Yet despite breaking
their covenant with God, Jews rarely enjoyed
equal status with their Christian neighbors, who
persisted in regarding them as untrustworthy out-
siders. The unstable identity of even the most assimilated Jew found poignant expression in the
accurate prediction of the famous German poet
and Christian convert, Heinrich Heine, "that at his
death neither mass nor *kaddish* would be said."[3]

Yasha Mazur—peripatetic, ambitious, Gentile-
looking, Polish-speaking—has implicitly accepted
the conditions for worldly success. Although he
continues to believe, his God is rather a nonsectar-
ian supreme artist adept at manipulating nature
than a partner in a uniquely Jewish covenant.
Yasha sheds what remains of his Jewish communal
identity after he kisses Esther good-bye on the outskirts of traditional Lublin. On the road his encounters with Magda the Gentile and Zeftel the
wayward Jewess prefigure the greater religious
dangers awaiting him in modern Warsaw. At the

end of his journey lies the prospect of full assimilation in marriage to Emilia. To the consummate role-player Emilia's price—conversion—seems little more than a costume change. Emilia appeals to Yasha's sense of his own worth as an artist: As her husband and a Christian he will gain the recognition he deserves on a wider stage than Poland. Their plan to run away to Italy reflects the greater freedom Yasha hopes to attain. Yet his insatiable appetite for freedom derives from his unfinished nature; Emilia's demands threaten to press upon him the fixed identity he has hitherto resisted. Before Yasha can turn back from Warsaw to Lublin, he must learn that both the freedom he has enjoyed and the new freedom held out by Emilia are illusory.

A first inkling that Yasha intuits the limits of freedom occurs near the beginning of *The Magician of Lublin* when, teasing Esther—"What would happen if I became an ascetic and, to repent, had myself bricked into a cell without a door?" (25)—he predicts the end of the novel. During the journey toward Warsaw evidence of Yasha's ambivalent attitude toward his own freedom sporadically crops up. His allusions to the piety of his late father and of his wife, his envy of the "unswerving faith" of traditional Jews, and his evident boredom with his chosen way of life all signal potential change. But it is the reawakening of covenantal memories that undercuts Yasha's freedom by keeping the spark of his Jewishness alive. On each of the three occasions when he takes refuge in a synagogue, Yasha is flooded with poignant reminders of his heritage. That sanctuary is to be found only in the synagogue among pious Jews is itself indicative of the direction Yasha must follow. Each encounter with traditional Judaism deepens his identification with a way of life he had ostensibly abandoned.

The first occurs on the road to Warsaw when Yasha ducks into a synagogue study house to escape a sudden rainstorm. There, amidst surroundings "strangely foreign to him, yet familiar," he feels the strength of the ties binding him to the Jewish community: "Its roots were his roots. He bore its mark upon his flesh" (67). Still, Yasha refuses phylacteries and prayer shawl, feeling obliged to rejoin Magda, who "had gone back to the wagon as if fearful of all this intense Jewishness." He is not yet prepared to acknowledge the synagogue as the locus of his primary obligation. Because he is traveling with a Gentile, Yasha poses as a Pole when they reach an inn. Run by Jews, the inn is "alive with Sabbath, holidays, the anticipation of the Messiah, and of the world to come." Magda and Yasha are served by a pious old Jewess who seemed "aware of a truth known only to

those not deceived by the vanity of worldly things"
(69). At the sight of her grandson's sidelocks and
fringed garment Yasha is nearly overcome: "Can I
forsake all this?" he asked himself. "This is mine
after all, mine. . . . Once I looked exactly like that
boy" (68–69).

Although Yasha's successive confrontations
with pious Jews, culminating in his self-
identification with the boy, have no immediate
consequences, they prove how indissoluble are his
ties to the Jewish community. And their lingering
effect may be apparent shortly after Yasha's arrival
in Warsaw, when his indecisive behavior with Emilia and his inability to rehearse for his forthcoming
engagement evidence a curious paralysis of will.
But two additional synagogue episodes are even
more decisive in shaping the resolution of Yasha's
identity crisis. After bungling his attempted rob-
bery, Yasha is driven by his pursuers to seek refuge
in the Gnoyne Street synagogue, where the beadle
puts into his hands the phylacteries and prayer
shawl which he had previously refused. Now,
however, they trigger a powerful series of epiphanies that culminate in renewed faith and reaffirmation of Jewish identity. At first he fumbles with the
unfamiliar implements of prayer. Then an old man
winds the phylacteries about Yasha's arm and ad-
justs the prayer shawl around his shoulders. A

sudden wave of brotherly love for his fellow worshipers, a feeling of shame for having betrayed his
heritage, and a remembrance of the promise to his
dying father that he would always remain a Jew
follow in rapid succession. With the return of his
"long-forgotten childhood devotion," the many
roles of Yasha the magician compress into one: "I
must be a Jew! . . . A Jew like all the others" (153).

These last words before leaving the synagogue
stabilize Yasha's identity but say nothing about its
maintenance. When he emerges from the protective gloom of the synagogue into the sunlight of
Gnoyne Street, it seems to Yasha that "the street
and the synagogue denied each other" (155). Because he is still unable to reconcile the conflicting
demands of religious and secular life, his doubts
reassert themselves. A third synagogue visit is required to clarify the meaning of his penitential
vows and to indicate the direction of his future life.
When he finds himself again at the door of the
Gnoyne Street synagogue a day later, it seems to
Yasha that God has guided his steps. It is the same
providence that prevented him from springing the
simple lock to Zaruski's safe, thereby causing him
to lose the money which would have won him
Emilia. With the revelation that everything comes
from God dawns the true meaning of Emilia's
"You must have some sort of a covenant with God

since he punishes you so promptly" (191). To Emilia, Yasha's punishment is presumably evidenced in the results of his bungled theft: loss of livelihood resulting from his damaged foot and loss of herself. In Singer's characteristic scheme of things, however, what Emilia takes for punishment actually constitutes salvation. By denying him the means to marry a Gentile, God has saved Yasha from the greatest loss of all—the loss of faith. Finally Yasha is able to understand the obligation enjoined upon him by virtue of the Jewish covenant with God: to keep to the path of righteousness by submitting to religious discipline. From this knowledge stems his eventual decision to end his tightrope-walking between tradition and assimilation by leading a life of piety in accordance with Jewish law.

Once the decision to serve God has been made, all that remains is to discover the form that service must take. Before leaving the synagogue Yasha opens a book to a verse from scripture: "He closeth his eyes not to see evil." To Yasha the apparently random act of choosing this particular book and opening it to this particular passage is proof positive of God's role in human affairs. This shift from his assumption that actions and events are products of chance to the orthodox Jewish position that nothing is coincidental marks an important stage in Yasha's spiritual development. Applying the scriptural lesson to his own life, he concludes that only intense discipline can curb his sinful instincts. The stronger the propensity toward sin, the more severe must be the discipline. Even before setting out from Lublin, Yasha revealed his awareness of this principle in his reply to Esther's claim that one could repent without being sealed into a cell: "It all depends on what sort of passion one is trying to control" (25). During the harrowing twenty-four hours that follow his last visit to the synagogue, the tragic consequences of his guilty passions reinforce his commitment to the life of religious discipline and dictate the radical mode of his penance.

Yasha's dark night of the soul commences with his discovery of Magda's suicide and ends with his sight of Zeftel in bed with the pimp Herman. The sleeping lovers, looking as if they "had been murdered," coalesce with the dead Magda and his likening of himself to a corpse to invoke in Yasha's mind Singer's habitual equation of lust with death. Staring at the "spent figures" of Zeftel and Herman and concluding that the preceding twenty-four hours had summed up his entire previous existence, Yasha the Magician metamorphoses into Jacob the Penitent. In the fate of Magda and Zeftel, Yasha reads his own. Only by withdrawing totally from the world can he abort the potentially evil consequences of his actions. Yet the imagery of death that triggers Yasha's renunciation applies not only to the folly of worldly striving but also to the futility of undisciplined freedom. And beyond Singer's implied doctrine that only the freedom conferred by religious belief is worthwhile lies his distrust of systems that would deny the "hand of God" in shaping Yasha's transformation.

Singer's fiction is philosophical in the sense of being rooted in a coherent system of belief—traditional Judaism—that serves as the measure of all things. Often his Jews are beleaguered by competing ideologies ranging from the religious heresy of Sabbatianism to the godless modern constructs of Darwinism, Marxism, and Freudianism. All are types of false messianism that play upon Jewish messianic yearnings; and all are dangerous because they dilute or displace traditional belief. In *The Magician of Lublin* existentialism joins the list of modern heresies that Singer condemns. While never explicitly defined as such, Yasha's is the classic existential drama acted out in the philosophical and literary works of Jean-Paul Sartre. Sartre's atheistic existentialism begins with the proposition that existence precedes essence. There is no essential human nature; rather, man is nothing else but the sum of his actions. Because he is nothing to begin with, he is indefinable until he makes something of himself. This definition, or lack of definition, places the entire responsibility for his existence upon the individual, whose awful freedom consists in the knowledge that he alone can give his life meaning. Neither God nor a set of commandments exists to legitimize human behavior. Lacking an abstract value system to fall back upon, man is solitary, without excuse, condemned to be free. Yasha Mazur is the Singer hero who comes closest to embodying Sartre's dictum that man *is* freedom.

Yasha's freedom, the subject of much envy early in *The Magician of Lublin,* is ironically reduced to worthlessness in the end. Yet until that fateful moment when the sight of Zeftel and Herman in bed signals the end of the road for its hero, *The Magician of Lublin* resembles an existential novel on the order of Sartre's *Nausea* (1938). Like Antoine Roquentin, the "hero" of *Nausea*—and the archetype of modern man—Yasha lives at a high metaphysical pitch, obsessed with uncovering the real secret of existence. Each flits from one role to the next, discovering only doubt and boredom in his many identities. Forced to confront the absurdity of their existence, Roquentin and Yasha are reduced in their suffering to nothing. Yasha's most acute symptoms of angst occur in the Warsaw streets. During his aimless flight from Zaruski's flat, and especially during his twenty-four-hour ordeal that culminates at the bedside of Zeftel and Herman, Yasha flails about in an existential sea. Flying from his pursuers down suddenly mysterious streets, searching unsuccessfully for once-familiar addresses, Yasha inhabits an increasingly surrealistic landscape that reflects the instability of his identity.

The terminology of existentialism—self-deception, absurdity, nothingness—applies no less to *The Magician of Lublin* than to *Nausea*. But their most striking resemblance results from invoking the felt horror of existence by the identical symptom: nausea. Fumbling with phylacteries and prayer shawl in the Gnoyne Street synagogue; riding in a *droshky* (coach) toward the scene of Magda's suicide; staggering from a tavern into the Warsaw streets, Yasha is overcome by waves of nausea. Most specifically during his *Walpurgisnacht* wanderings that take Yasha from Magda's suicide to Zeftel's betrayal, Warsaw assumes the funereal aspect of Roquentin's Bouville. These hellish settings are the objective correlatives of the emotional states expressed by nausea. Grime, heat, and stench pervade the crowded streets down which Yasha stumbles, finally to emerge on Castle Place. A sulfurous breeze and a glowing sky, loitering prostitutes, reeling drunkards, and festering corpses complete a picture of Warsaw become hell. Here Yasha suffers the last and most severe of his attacks of nausea: "He belched and tasted an unfamiliar bitterness. I know, it's the world" (213). Arising from the horror of his own existence to embrace the world and all its people, Yasha's revulsion reflects his self-deception. As a result of failing to act authentically, Yasha is reduced to nothing. Far from being resolved, his identity crisis has grown so acute as to render all roles and actions equally implausible. Near the end of *Nausea* a scrap of jazz suggests to Roquentin the saving grace of art, the glimmer of hope that through his writing he can achieve an authentic identity. That the existential dilemma cannot be solved by art— or by any other secular panacea—is the lesson of *The Magician of Lublin*. Yasha is already the consummate artist. Yet there seems to be nothing intrinsically sacrosanct about art itself. Yasha's restlessness and boredom; his constant search for novelty, expressed in ever more risky stunts; and his paralysis before his Warsaw opening indicate the limitations of art. Confronted with the simple lock on Zaruski's safe, Yasha's art suddenly deserts him; not only does he fail to open the lock, but he loses his skeleton key and carelessly leaves behind some pages from his address book. Climbing down from Zaruski's balcony, the brilliant acrobat and tightrope walker tries to support himself on the shoulders of a statue—"but his feet lacked their usual sureness," and he drops to the ground, injuring his foot. The comically bungled crime at Zaruski's flat ironically punctures the inflated balloon of art that Sartre lofts in the concluding pages of *Nausea.* A passage in Singer's memoirs alludes to his own misplaced efforts "to become a priest of this idolatry, although I was aware of its falsehood. At its best, art could be nothing more than a means of forgetting the human disaster for a while."[4]

Singer's criticism of art reflects his overall methodology in *The Magician of Lublin:* to poison the very concept of freedom by exhibiting its evil effects. He takes the orthodox position that the world is *tref,* and that such uncleanness must result from the exercise of human freedom, since God could not create an evil world. It then follows that freedom itself is suspect, particularly when it operates outside the boundaries fixed by religious discipline. Even if Sartre's vision of a godless world were accurate, man would have to invent God in order to create a moral context for his actions. Unable to share Sartre's essentially sanguine outlook on human nature, Singer argues that only the hope—or fear—of an afterlife persuades man voluntarily to set limits on his freedom. For Singer's Jew those limits were long ago fixed in place by an ancient system of belief. As a Jew, Yasha can act authentically only by adhering to the Jewish belief system which alone is capable of conferring a meaningful identity upon him. His decision to repent involves, therefore, the surrender of the specious freedom that has defined him and the assumption of the stable identity that he has so long resisted. In a typically didactic Singer epilogue Yasha's version of Jewish identity threatens to raise as many questions as it answers about punishment, repentance, free will, and Judaism itself.

Three years after his return to Lublin signaled the end of his life in the world, Yasha has had himself bricked into a doorless hut whose one tiny window provides his only outside contact. While his sincerity is evident—renamed Jacob the Penitent, he has reverted to traditional sidelocks and dress and reads the Torah endlessly—his radical mode of penance risks parodying Jewish identity. The unintentional flamboyance of a way of life that attracts the pious and the idly curious alike evokes unbidden memories of Yasha's earlier role-playing. The rigor of his chosen punishment seems unjustified by any correspondingly serious crime. Jacob the Penitent denies life, first by willfully separating himself from his wife and his community, then by lobotomizing his free will. What Esther calls his prison effectively dampens Yasha's sinful instincts, but only at the cost of canceling familial and communal obligations as the traditional determinants of Jewish identity. Unwittingly Yasha may be sapping the power of his renewed covenant with God by neglecting the human relationships on which that covenant depends. Because God's pact is not with a single person but with a chosen people, Yasha's extreme form of penitence runs the risk of dangerously oversimplifying Jewish covenantal bonding.

The traditional Jewish objection to Yasha's immurement is voiced in the rabbi's reminder that God created the world "for the exercise of free will. . . . Man deprived of free will was like a corpse"(223). If man cannot freely choose to abstain from evil, then his life has no meaning. Ironically, this traditional Jewish line is analogous to Sartre's dictum that man *is* freedom. But Yasha has already exercised his freedom—with disastrous results. Believing himself responsible for Magda's suicide and Zeftel's prostitution, he is convinced that only by total imprisonment can he atone for his sins and guard against their recurrence. Beset by strong passions, Yasha can envision no middle ground between absolute freedom and living en-

tombment; he asserts the last vestige of his freedom in disavowing freedom itself. Unable to serve
both God and man, Yasha has done the next best
thing, exchanging a life of meaningless and destructive freedom for one of slavery to God. The
ultimate interpretation of his radical penance is
ambiguous. Imprisoned in his cell, he finds that
his outward metamorphosis into Jacob the Penitent
is accompanied by no corresponding inward
change. He is prevented from sinning, but the
temptation to sin endures. Thus Yasha's bizarre
decision may result less from his conviction of its
penitential fitness than from his sad recognition of
human depravity. Still, it is one thing to acknowledge depravity, quite another to deny the human
capacity for transcending it. Although Yasha opts
out of the Jewish drama of moral choice, he is sufficiently redeemed by the purity of his motives to
earn the rabbi's blessing: "Your actions are in-
tended for the glory of Heaven. May the Almighty
help you!" (223).

The Penitent

The Penitent, serialized in the *Forward* in 1974
and published in English ten years later, is Singer's
contemporary recasting of his theme of returning

to Jewish roots. Its Yiddish title, *Der Baal Tschuve*, refers to its protagonist, Joseph Shapiro, who explains that "*Baal Tschuve* means one who returns. I came back home."[5] These words were addressed to Singer during his 1969 visit to Jerusalem as he stands looking at the famous Wailing Wall. A surviving section of the ancient enclosure of Herod's temple, the "Wall is like a magnet that draws Jewish souls" (5). As the place where Jews traditionally gather for prayer and for religious lament, the Wall is the symbolic repository of those values that Joseph seeks. Although he arrived in Israel by air, Joseph's is the same penitential journey to a spiritual destination formerly taken by Jacob in *The Slave* and by Yasha in *The Magician of Lublin*. Again Singer's focus is upon an individual, not an epoch; yet it is in large part Joseph's perception of the modern world that influences his decision to repent.

Penitential decisions most often arise from a sense of self-loathing, itself induced by mounting proof of personal waywardness. Only when the force of the evidence grows insurmountable is the desire to repent fully translated into the sort of penitential action that drives Yasha Mazur into a cell and Joseph Shapiro into the ultraorthodox Meah Shearim section of Jerusalem. Apparently unrelated actions assume the pattern of a sinful way of life, a pattern apprehended in critical moments of insight or introspection. There is no shortage of epiphanies in *The Penitent*. Like those in *The Magician of Lublin*, they are frequently triggered by episodes of sexual disenchantment. Joseph's most intense shock of recognition—the discovery of his wife, Celia, in bed with another man—closely parallels Yasha's—the sight of Zeftel in bed with Herman. While these recognition scenes are decisive in turning sinners into penitents, their apparently similar effects threaten to camouflage the psychological gulf separating their principal actors. Seeing Zeftel with Herman shocks Yasha into fully comprehending the role of personal responsibility in human relationships. And it is from a profound sense of his own culpability in the tragic fates of Zeftel and Magda that his decision to repent derives. Yasha's turning from the world is an acknowledgment of its corruption; but more importantly, it is an admission of his own share in making the world corrupt. No such admission results from Joseph's discovery of Celia's infidelity. Rather, he attributes this and similar misfortunes to his surroundings, so that the penitential tale he unfolds to Singer is not so much a confession of personal shortcomings as a diatribe against the modern world.

Women bear the brunt of Joseph's attack, since

unsatisfactory sexual relationships are at the root
of his disenchantment. Typically, he blames his
sordid affair with the avaricious divorcée Liza
on the modern world, which tempts men by hatch-
ing such women. Celia's adultery—conceivably
prompted by his neglect—provides the excuse for
another of Joseph's antifeminist diatribes. In his
consummate hypocrisy he frequently alludes to
her "guilt." When he imagines the trouble of get-
ting a divorce and the amount of alimony he may
be forced to pay, he denounces "the Gentile and
the Jewish-Gentile laws—they favor the guilty"
(97). Younger women fare no better. Micki, Liza's
daughter, is a caricature of radical 1960s youth.
Pregnant by her brutish left-wing lover, clamoring
for Joseph to finance her abortion, and violently
attacking her mother, Micki epitomizes for Joseph
the younger generation. Her more sophisticated
and intelligent, but no less contemptible, counterpart is Priscilla, whose unfaithfulness to her fiancé
and casual promiscuity with Joseph aboard their
flight to Israel display the brazenness of "a depraved female who would give herself to any-
body" (82). Celia and Liza are lumped together as
lovers of pornographic books, gangster movies,
lobster, and "plays full of shocking horror and dissolution" done "in the name of an art whose eternal theme is violence and fornication" (124). Such

ranting makes up the greater part of Joseph's monologue and embodies the methodology of *The Penitent:* to fasten upon any excuse for denouncing the
modern world. While its scope and virulence
threaten to devalue it as serious criticism, there
can be little doubt that Joseph's interminable jere-
miad reflects Singer's views. These are made apparent in the author's note, which cites "the lack
of dignity and the degradation of modern man, his
precarious family life, his greed for luxury and
gadgets, his disdain of the old, his obesiance before the young, his blind faith in psychiatry, his
ever-growing tolerance of crime."

Orthodox Hasidim alone are exempt from the
sweeping denunciations of a sermon that might
better have been preached by Pinhos-Mendel,
Singer's pious father. Only in the Hasidic prayer
house that precariously survives on New York's
Lower East Side and among the ultraorthodox in
the Meah Shearim sector of Jerusalem does Joseph
feel safe from the doubts that plague him. So powerful and unceasing are the onslaughts of modernity that the penitent must grow a beard and
sidelocks and wear a ritual garment to be called a
real Jew. Joseph comes to believe that this "uni-
form" of God's soldiers provides the only armor
against temptation. This extravagant claim is con-
sistent with his view that contact with the modern

world dries up the wellsprings of faith. Like Yasha Mazur, Joseph feels that he must wall out the world if he is to avoid transgressing. Neither as sinner nor as penitent does either possess full faith; both exemplify Joseph's belief that "deeds must come first. . . . Jewishness leads to faith" (161). Marriage to Sarah, the shy and chaste daughter of his Hasidic host, is, like the assumption of traditional dress, one of those deeds that confer full Jewishness upon Joseph. Sarah, whose voice is that of an "obedient child," and whose fecundity contrasts with Celia's barrenness, is Singer's ideal Jewish woman, in every respect the antithesis of the modern liberated female.

So depraved is the modern world that Joseph can repent only by embracing a way of life anchored in the past. Modern Jews fare no better than Gentiles in *The Penitent*: Tel Aviv is as tainted by modernity as New York, London, or Paris. It is not to modern Judaism that the prospective penitent must return, but "to the Jewishness of grandfathers and great-grandfathers" (42). Because quotidian life is as relentlessly erased by the past as by a cell, Joseph's penitence effectively resembles Yasha's. And both penitents, fearing the consequences of their actions, seek a final escape from the human dilemma that, in Singer's words, "would void the greatest gift that God has bestowed upon mankind—free choice." By refusing to "look history in the face and to accept it as a terrifying dialogue with Yahweh,"[6] Joseph and Yasha deny the Jewish messianic vision. Their radical forms of penance unwittingly threaten to mimic heretical Sabbatian attempts to hasten the end of history. One day the true Messiah will appear and history will be duly abolished. Until that day, however, "historical events have a value in themselves, insofar as they are determined by the will of God"; and "history must be tolerated only because it is known that, one day or another, it will cease."[7]

Far more than *The Magician of Lublin, The Penitent* is marked by unwillingness to tolerate history. As the archetypal Holocaust survivor who fled Poland in 1939, wandered through Stalin's war-torn Russia, and landed by virtue of a visa mixup in America, Joseph has ample reason to hate history. Some of his most outrageous comparisons—humanists with Hitler, assimilated Jews with Nazis—may arise from an understandable tendency to identify modernity by its most horrifying phenomena. Joseph's desperate identification with the remnants of Hasidic Jewry results not so much from religious fanaticism as from the lack of communal alternatives. To achieve Hitler's goal of a *judenrein* (Jew free) Europe, the Nazi war against the Jews focused on Poland, eventually wiping out all but a tiny percentage of Europe's largest Jewish population. After World War II, the sort of Lublin Jewish community to which Yasha returned to do penance no longer existed. Nor does its counterpart exist in America, where Jewish homelessness and marginality assumed the dubious status of sociological and literary clichés. In *The Penitent* the handful of Hasidic worshipers who gather together on the Lower East Side comprise New York's only viable Jewish community. What remains of prewar communal Judaism has been symbolically reduced to a roomful of aged and infirm Hasidim best represented by their rabbi, himself a miraculous survivor of the Maidenek concentration camp. That the rabbi has no apparent successor—his children perished in Europe— and that Joseph's presence is required to fill out a *minyan* (the ten adult males needed for prayer)—is a sad reminder of Jewish loss and an ill omen for Jewish continuity.

Joseph's sudden departure from New York to seek in Israel what he finds missing in America is the by-product of instinctive assumptions that history has rendered obsolete. Due to the very success that transformed the dream of a Jewish homeland into the reality of a Jewish national state, modern Israel is nearly indistinguishable from other countries. Even Hebrew, the language

of piety, has debased itself by coining words for
frivolous modern gadgets and fashions. Spotting
advertisements for "kitsch novels" and "cheap
plays" translated into the Holy Tongue, Joseph
sadly concludes: "We are a people like all other
peoples. We feed ourselves the same dung as they
do" (99). His words condemn far more than the
vulgarity of modern art. Joseph's contempt for
Jews who act like Gentiles goes to the heart of the
age-old Jewish fear of extinction, and a long way
toward justifying the radical mode of his penance.
An inevitable aspect of Jewish consciousness, such
fear grows pervasive after the Holocaust and accounts in large part for a dramatic shift in post-
Holocaust Jewish thought.

Fear of extinction, cruelly exacerbated by a
Holocaust that devastated European Jewry, did not
entirely subside in its wake. Assimilation became a
dirty word to many Jews, especially Holocaust survivors, who feared that American freedom would
prolong the nightmare of annihilation initiated by
Nazi persecution. As long ago as the 1880s, when
masses of East European Jews emigrated to America, their image of a *goldene medine* (golden land)
was clouded by the suspicion that Jewish belief
could not be sustained in the New World. Until the
Holocaust drastically reduced Jewish numbers and
shifted the center of Jewish life from the old world

to the new, assimilation was mostly a family tragedy (or triumph), the stuff of countless fictional
treatments of generational conflict. After the Holocaust, the arithmetic of Jewish losses to assimilation had to be recalculated; and the incalculable
"success" of assimilation had to be dreaded. Ostensibly liberal Jewish American writers co-opted
the antiassimilationist arguments of the queru-
lously orthodox. Philip Roth evokes the crisis of
Jewish identity brought on by assimilation and material prosperity in "Eli the Fanatic" (1959). The
eponymous hero of Roth's story, at first embar-
rassed by the sudden appearance of Hasidic survivors of the Holocaust in his fashionable suburb,
ends by trading his Brooks Brothers suit for an Hasidic caftan. Eli's willing assumption of full Jewish
identity seals his brotherhood with all Jews and
defines a strategy for preserving traditional values
in a secular culture.

   While Singer's is a lifelong antipathy toward
assimilation, the virulence of Joseph's contempt
for Jews who are "like all other peoples" owes
something to the historical context of *The Penitent*.
The late 1960s and early 1970s seem in retrospect a
period when fears of assimilation were aggravated
by growing reservations about American society.
Secular humanism in its 1960s American incarna-
tion is amoral and devoid of intellectual substance

THE PENITENT

in Saul Bellow's *Mr. Sammler's Planet* (1970). Mr. Sammler, a Polish Jewish intellectual who miraculously survived the Holocaust, has witnessed the failure of the universal, liberal, and progressive theories he once espoused. Their final defeat—epitomized by the moral and intellectual wasteland of contemporary New York—triggers Sammler's acceptance of Jewish tradition as the guide for human action. For Singer's Joseph Shapiro, whose attacks on modernity are both more strident and less elegant than Mr. Sammler's, that tradition survives authentically only in such pious enclaves as Meah Shearim. Joseph's new way of life is mandated by overpowering modern challenges to Jewish identity. Safe from outside pressures and temptations in Meah Shearim, he does penance not only as an act of atonement for his sins, but as a strategy for maintaining Jewish identity in the modern world. What began as a gesture of personal renunciation turns into a paradigm for Jewish communal living.

Notes

1. Isaac Bashevis Singer, *The Magician of Lublin* (New York: Noonday Press, 1960) 58. Page references in parentheses are to this edition.

2. Lucy Dawidowicz, *The Jewish Presence: Essays on Identity and History* (New York: Harcourt Brace, 1978) 10.

3. Alan L. Berger, *Crisis and Covenant: The Holocaust in American Jewish Fiction* (Albany: State University of New York Press, 1985) 8.

4. Singer, *Love and Exile* (Garden City, NY: Doubleday, 1984) 347.

5. Singer, *The Penitent* (New York: Farrar, Straus, 1983) 5. Page references in parentheses are to this edition.

6. Mircea Eliade, *The Myth of the Eternal Return* (New York: Pantheon, 1954) 108.

7. Eliade 104, 111. For Eliade, messianic belief underlies the crucial Jewish discovery of "the meaning of history as the epiphany of God."

CHAPTER FIVE

Enemies, A Love Story and *Shosha*

Although Singer has lived the greater part of his life in the United States, his fictional subjects remain the Yiddish-speaking Jews of Poland. Whatever the role of the Jewish community, its very existence is indispensable to those novels set before 1939. After the Holocaust destroyed their world, and with it Singer's natural setting, his people grow more fragile, his themes more tentative. In his author's note to *Enemies*, Singer resists historical determinism: "The characters are not only Nazi victims but victims of their own personalities and fates." Yet history has stamped upon them, as indelible as a concentration camp tattoo, a new identity—survivor. And by erasing Jewish communal life it has deflected or displaced Singer's cardinal theme of penitence. The more contemporary the setting, the more omnipresent the Holocaust and the more likely are Yiddish-speaking Jews to be survivors. Joseph Shapiro (*The Penitent*) and Aaron Greidinger (*Shosha*) are survivors by virtue of escaping Poland before the Holocaust. Among the protagonists of Singer's novels only Herman Broder (*Enemies*) spends World War II entirely in Poland; and only in *Enemies* is narrative strategy and outcome so relentlessly determined by the Holocaust and its aftermath.

Given the facts of Singer's origin and upbringing, it is inevitable that the Holocaust looms large in his fiction. Unlike his American Jewish counterparts he is condemned by his subject matter to confront the Holocaust endlessly. Only *Satan in Goray* was written before the Holocaust, and premonitions of disaster abound even in this earliest of his novels. Such premonitions, grown terrifyingly precise with passing time, unite with Holocaust imagery to cast a pall over Polish Jewry from the seventeenth century until the Nazi invasion of 1939. Atrocities open and close Singer's chronology of Jewish life in Poland: Hitler's program of genocide is the end product of a process dating from Chmielnicki's pogroms. Nor is there any guarantee that anti-Semitism and the persecution it engenders will not flare up again, even in America. The Holocaust survivors of *Enemies* are ravaged by nightmares of Nazi pursuit. Herman Broder nervously eyes possible hiding places in case of a German invasion of New York, and Masha half expects Nazis to show up in the Catskills. Herman understandably sees the present in the past: "Cain continues to murder Abel. Nebuchadnezzar is still slaughtering the sons of Zedekiah and putting out Zedekiah's eyes. The pogrom in Kesheniev never ceases. Jews are forever being burned in Auschwitz."[1] This grim and hopeless vision of eternal slaughter encapsulates Singer's view of history as eternal recurrence. The more remote the action of a novel from the Holocaust, the greater the prospect of mining traces of hope from history's endless repetitions. Crossing the Vistula in the seventeenth-century world of *The Slave,* Jacob reenacts the role—fraught with the promise of Jewish continuity—of his biblical namesake. Still, even that affirmation of God's design is accompanied by an "ancient grief." The product of a historical epoch in which, at least for Jacob, Jews remain beneficiaries of God's providence, no such optimism is warranted in an era which produces the Holocaust. Modern times spawn a revisionist theory of ever-recurring cycles of history that was never very far below the surface of even the most sanguine interpretations of Jewish destiny. The Holocaust renders divine providence fatally suspect. This latest and most terrible evidence that God has averted His face from Jewish suffering inspires Herman Broder's nihilistic reading of his people's history. Singer's memoirs invoke the fateful moment that sealed his own loss of faith. On a train bound for Warsaw and his new job as proofreader of the *Literary Pages,* he "had opportunity to witness the depths of human degradation, of Jewish anguish." Polish hooligans abuse and attack "ragged" and "broken" Jews, provoking the nineteen-year-old Singer to laugh at his own illusions: "I knew what I was seeing now was the essence of human history."[2] Already in 1923 Singer draws the inevitable conclusion: that eternal cycles of history promise endless Jewish suffering.

Enemies, a Love Story—serialized in the *Forward* in 1966 and published in English in 1972—is the first of Singer's novels to be set in the post-Holocaust world. While the heroes of his two later works are also Polish-Jewish survivors, *The Penitent* and *Shosha* treat the Holocaust only tangentially. Neither Joseph Shapiro nor Aaron Greidinger seems fashioned primarily by his wartime experiences. Even Herman Broder "had been a victim long before Hitler's day"; yet his "sorrow that could not be assuaged," while not engendered by the Nazis, is shaped and intensified by the Holocaust. "Anyone who's gone through all I have is no longer a part of this world" (25), explains Herman, justifying his reclusive behavior to his employer, Rabbi Lampert. "Clichés, empty words," retorts the rabbi, unwittingly disclosing the unbridgeable chasm separating Holocaust survivors like Herman from those who passed the war safely in America, like himself. That Herman remains the same man he was before the war—"a fatalistic hedonist who lived in presuicidal gloom"—and that he is not above invoking the Holocaust to condone his own amorality, strips his endemic irresponsibility of its protective camouflage. In Singer's complex portrait Herman is at once an innocent victim and a heedless victimizer. So strong is the sense of victimization in *Enemies* that Herman not only refuses to eat flesh but gets up in the middle of the night to free mice from Masha's traps. Because all of its principal characters are victims of the Holocaust, *Enemies* falls into that important subgenre of Jewish literature dedicated to remembrance. Even more critical then the task of memorializing the world of prewar Jewry is the sacred duty of bearing witness to its annihilation. Among Hitler's countless victims were those whose burning desire to record the greatest infamy in human history may partially explain their survival. To their records, which consist mainly of diaries and retrospective memoirs, must be added a growing body of fiction like *Enemies* which seeks to re-create their experiences. Herman's wife, Tamara; his mistress, Masha; and Masha's mother, Shifrah Puah, survived both ghettos and concentration camps, the archetypal hells of Jewish incarceration and extermination.

Singer's Holocaust survivors can never forget. Eyewitnesses to the slaughter of their people, Tamara, Masha, and Shifrah Puah are compulsive retellers of their stories. What identity they possess derives from their role as survivors: "It is Hitler who has defined the modern Jew and continues to define him from the grave."[3] The three women survive as the sum of their Holocaust experiences. As in Herman's case, their personalities were not forged in the crucible of the Holocaust; but the Holocaust impinges so cruelly upon their present lives as to negate them. Ghosts of their former selves, they can only relive the past and despair of the future. Shifrah Puah's "Whoever has tasted death has no more use for life" (36) applies in varying degrees to Masha and Tamara as well. All three bear the guilt of their own survival and the stigmata of Nazi-hatred. The bayonet scar on Shifrah Puah's cheek, the inability of Masha to bear children, and the bullet lodged in Tamara's body are permanent souvenirs of their sojourn in hell. Each woman's response to her experience of the

Holocaust represents a version of Jewish survival. Shifrah Puah believes that God took all the pious Jews and that she survives only because of her sins; Tamara, comfortable in her room in New York, imagines that she has "betrayed all the Jews in Europe." Shifrah Puah, called "back from the other world" by Masha, and Tamara, returned from the dead, derive great moral authority by virtue of their "resurrection." Even the cynical Herman admits that everything that Shifrah Puah touches is "holy," and that whatever Tamara says must be believed. Tamara's uncle, Reb Abraham Nissen Yaroslaver, who fled to America only weeks before Hitler's invasion of Poland, claims special status for all Holocaust survivors. To this pious Hasid, whose own faith has been shaken, anyone who had witnessed the carnage has reason not to "believe in The Almighty and in His mercy" (245).

The conflict between faith and doubt that plagues Reb Abraham Nissen extends to nearly every major character in *Enemies*. While it is true that the problem of belief dominates all of Singer's fiction, it is particularly critical in the post-Holocaust era. As always, the clash between belief and denial is reflected in his protagonist's inner life. Herman Broder is another of Singer's moral schizophrenics who wish to believe but are unable to do so. Like earlier Singer heroes whose compulsive womanizing stems from alienation, Herman employs hedonism as a mode of evasion. By multiplying their sexual partners, they devour time which might otherwise be spent in grappling with the problem of leading meaningful lives. Asa Heshel (*The Family Moskat*) and Yasha Mazur (*The Magician of Lublin*) are forever shuttling between assignations, hailing droshkies, awaiting streetcars, even walking from one end of Warsaw to the other when all else fails. It is no coincidence that Singer locates Herman's three wives so far apart, forcing Herman to spend hours riding subways between Brooklyn and the Bronx. Among Singer's hedonistic protagonists Herman leads the most complicated life precisely because he has the greatest need to conquer time by canceling it. His love life aside, Herman exhibits the same near-paralysis that sporadically overtakes Asa Heshel and Yasha. Indeed, Herman is Asa Heshel reincarnated in his alienation from God and his helplessness without God. Former Talmud students, they have bartered the Jewish world view for a theory that sees in lust the common denominator of human behavior. Yet neither gains lasting satisfaction from sexual relationships. Each carelessly spawns children he doesn't want and effectively denies. Asa Heshel callously abandons the two wives who have borne his son and daughter; Herman routinely betrays three wives and wastes remarkably little emotion on his dead children.

Children are conspicuously absent from *Enemies* but are unfailingly invoked in the Holocaust stories of the major characters. Jewish childhood, rarely happy in the best of times, epitomizes the tragic dimensions of Jewish suffering during the Holocaust. Jewish self-definition historically centers upon children, from whom parents derive *naches* (pleasure) and *koved* (honor and esteem). To an endlessly besieged people children represent the only hope of continuity, so much so that reproduction is enjoined upon traditional Jews as a sacred duty. The murder of children was therefore the most devastating aspect of Hitler's war against the Jews, for "in making certain that their children would be ash, the Germans deprived human history of one of the versions of its future. Genocide is the ultimate crime because it pre-empts on the future, because it tears up one of the roots from which history grows."[4] A shattering epiphany of the destroyed family and the foreclosed future bursts upon Eugenia Ginzburg as she awaits transport to the sort of Soviet camp that Tamara barely survived. Commanded to give up the pictures of their children, Ginzburg and the other women pile them on the stone floor of the prison yard: "One of the warders had to cross the yard and, rather than walk around the pile, stamped straight across the faces of our children. I saw his foot in close-up, as though it were in a film."[5] Holocaust survivors are ambivalent about children, torn between the desire to restore Jewish losses and the fear of bringing innocents into an evil world. Shifrah Puah wants a grandchild, "someone to name after the murdered Jews" (184), and Yadwiga finally bears Herman's child. But the former is a saint, the latter a Gentile. More typical of the reactions of Singer's Holocaust survivors to the prospect of childbearing is Tamara's "What for? So that the Gentiles will have someone to burn?" (101). Yadwiga's pregnancy is, of course, accidental: "Herman took care not to make Yadwiga pregnant. In a world in which one's children could be dragged away from their mother and shot, one had no right to have more children" (7). It is significant that on the eve of the High Holy Days with their promise of Jewish renewal, Herman admits that "of all his fears, the greatest was his fear of again becoming a father" (149). Herman's nihilism finds its most obsessive expression in his revulsion against children, as if by refusing to procreate he might abolish the creation he finds so depraved.

Theories about the inherent evil of human nature, ever present in Singer's fiction, crop up incessantly in *Enemies*. The Singer novel most directly concerned with the Holocaust, *Enemies* naturally contains some of his most bitter reflections on the human condition. Expanding the horror stories of Holocaust survivors into general conclusions about human nature is the task of several otherwise gratuitous passages. Typical of these is the long monologue delivered by Masha's former husband, Leon Tortshiner, during his meeting with Herman in a cafeteria. Ostensibly a tip-off about Masha's infidelities, Tortshiner's speech abstracts from her scandalous conduct a favorite Singer theory about the degeneration of the human species: "I believe, so to speak, in an evolution in reverse. The last man on earth will be both a criminal and a madman" (163). Such theories reflect Singer's view of history as cyclical nightmare and the Holocaust as the unholy paradigm of human action. More devastating even than their conclusions about human nature are their implications about the nature of God. Even the pious Reb Abraham Nissen cannot accept the position of orthodox Jews, "who tried to pretend that the Holocaust in Europe had never taken place" (245). A variation on this theme—that the Holocaust, like previous disasters, was visited upon the Jewish people by God as punishment for their sins—is equally unacceptable to the major characters in *Enemies*. For Herman, Masha, and Tamara the Holocaust is evidence that God has broken His covenant with His chosen people. Their several theories mirror the belief, commonly held by survivors, that at the very least God averted His face from the Jews in their time of greatest need; at the worst, He willed their destruction. "Almighty sadist," Herman calls God (205). "Jews must be slaughtered—that's what God wants," cries Masha (37). Both consider the possibility that Hitler presides in heaven, or that if a merciful God exists, "then he was only a helpless godlet, a kind of heavenly Jew among the heavenly Nazis" (123). Tamara's suffering and the murder of her children have convinced her that "the merciful God in whom we believed does not exist" (81). The sight of children going "to their deaths like saints" proves only that "souls exist; it's God who doesn't" (82–83). If history, as represented archetypally by the Holocaust, conforms to a divine blueprint, then it constitutes a shattering indictment of God. Either God is present in history and is therefore cruel or unfeeling; or He is absent from history and is therefore nonexistent or dead.

In the wake of the Holocaust doubts about the nature and existence of God raise the possibility that the vaunted covenant between God and His chosen people is a macabre hoax. Or the covenant may be the product of wishful thinking, the at-

tempt of a desperate people to foist upon God a
responsibility for history in general and for Jewish
survival in particular that He is unready or unwilling to assume. God looks the other way during the
Holocaust to signal His refusal to engage in a dialogue, much less to sign a contract, with a people
whom He has not chosen but who have chosen
Him. Masha claims that Hitler carried out God's
diabolical plan to destroy the Jews: "The true God
hates us, but we have dreamed up an idol who
loves us and has made us His chosen people. . . .
the Gentile makes gods of stone and we of theories" (110). An analogous view of Judaism as a
fragile and artificial construct surfaces in Herman's
metaphor: "a hothouse growth . . . kept thriving
in an alien environment nourished by the belief in
a Messiah, the hope of justice to come, the promise of the Bible—the Book that had hypnotized
them forever" (52). Masha and Herman define the
essential unreality of a religion created from theories and books. It is just such a reliance on words
that contributes to the Jewish condition that Hannah Arendt, one of the most profound political
thinkers of the twentieth century, describes as
worldlessness. The key feature of modern Jewish
history for Arendt, worldlessness stems from the
Jewish strategy of ensuring survival by dissociating
from the dominant Christian society. Successful

up to a point, this same strategy that sustained the Jewish community left it politically debilitated. Ignorant of conditions in the real world, Jews were slow to recognize threats to their survival and powerless to meet them. Hitler's "terrible and bloody annihilation of individual Jews was preceded by the bloodless destruction of the Jewish people."[6] Arendt's conclusions are implicit in the contentions of Masha and Herman that Jews have been betrayed by books. That Singer leaves the door to this interpretation ajar is evidence of the despair engendered by the Holocaust.

Jewish denial of the world, regarded so negatively by Arendt, is construed paradoxically by Singer. To the extent that it is a political phenomenon, worldlessness threatens Jewish survival; to the extent that it is a religious phenomenon, it constitutes Judaism's only hope of survival. A Singer novel invariably establishes a context in which Jewishness is enervated or extinguished through contact with the world. Worldliness, signaled by changes in moral outlook and symbolized by changes in dress, is tantamount in its extreme form to assimilation or even to conversion. Although Herman is hardly unworldly, he is revolted by the Americanized Jews whose hijinks in the Catskills "shamed the agony of the holocaust" (121). Tamara regards her old self as dead, her new self a vulgar parody of what she once was: "They put nylon stockings on me, dyed my hair, and polished my fingernails, God help me, but Gentiles have always prettied up their corpses, and Jews nowadays are Gentiles" (77). Her belief cauterized by the Nazis, Tamara nevertheless resists attempts to distort her Jewish identity. Herman and Masha, who regard themselves as Jews in name only, take turns confessing to the persistence of belief. First Herman hesitates to abandon the pregnant Yadwiga for Masha: "I'm afraid of God" (252). Later Masha refuses to leave her dead mother unburied to run away with Herman, fearing to "be damned for ten generations to come" (274). Haunted by echoes from a former life, these two apostles of unbridled hedonism react as Jews in moments of crisis.

This clash between belief and disbelief forms the central drama of any Singer novel. So long as Poland, its Jewish community intact, is the scene of that drama, details of appearance and dress denote varying degrees of religious observance. Such outward badges of belief lose their referential power in post-Holocaust New York, where Singer's Jews are refugee survivors and Judaism lacks communal definition. Herman lives among Jews but denies their relevance as a community. To Herman and to most of his fellow survivors Jewish communal life terminated in the Holocaust. The postwar atomization of Jewry, so evident in *Enemies,* dictates a modified strategy for dramatizing the crisis of belief. Jewishness comes to be reckoned more by words than by mannerisms, more by inward states than by outward actions. In moments of deepest despair Herman rejects the words that express the Jewish covenant with God. Meanings of words grow distorted or negated as Herman and Masha conceive the covenant to be an ironic artifact of wishful Jewish forging, or the death warrant delivered by an uncaring or hostile God. In their view God's words to the Jews promise no more than those of the Nazis, who, in Masha's grimmest scenario, were simply following His orders. The wrenching of the German language prefigured the persecution of the Jews. Adolf Eichmann, coordinating the transport of millions to concentration camps, talked about "processing" Jews. Those destined for extermination were referred to as "pieces," "specimens," "material" by murderers whose disposal of people was expedited by reducing them to things. Even in death Jewish victims were denied human status. Thrown into vast unmarked ditches, their corpses became *lumpen* (rags) or *puppen* (dolls). Yet Herman's cynicism about God's covenant and God's intentions stops just short of total denial. As often as he doubts God's word, Herman reaffirms it. During the many times when he reverts to his Talmudic upbringing and vows to "spit in the face of worldliness," he equates repentance with utter faithfulness to the letter of Jewish law. At night, unable to sleep, he realizes that he can escape from the mutual deception of his relationship with Masha only by going "back to the Torah, the Gemara, the Jewish books." Herman's various moods are reflected in his fluctuating commitment to the word of God as revealed by holy scripture. When his resolve to repent flags, he stares at the neglected volumes of the Gemara (the Babylonian Talmud) gathering dust on the shelves of his bookcase. But at those moments when he seems most determined to repent, he takes down his books: "He sat over his Gemara, staring at the letters, at the words. These writings were home. On these pages dwelt his parents, his grandparents, all his ancestors" (172).

Singer's symbolic use of words in *Enemies* is a reminder that Judaism is, above all, a religion of the word. For orthodox Jews reality is grounded not in the visible world, but in holy scripture. Nature is regarded as alien, if not hostile—a Gentile purview. The prematurely aged *heder* boy poring endlessly over the Talmud is a stock figure in Yiddish literature. Singer occasionally goes so far as to equate physical imperfections with piety and glowing health with apostasy. All but a few of his pious women, no matter their age, are wizened crones; and the Jewishness of such robust figures as Gediliya (*Satan in Goray*) and Yasha Mazur (*The Magician of Lublin*) is immediately suspect. Such is their dependence on the word for sustenance that Jews deprived of their books fear loss of identity. Jacob, lacking books in captivity, holds on to his Jewishness in *The Slave* by repeating over and over again pages and entire chapters of scripture that he had once committed to memory. Singer's penitents invariably surround themselves with holy books as shields against worldliness. Like them, Herman concludes that "if a Jew departed so much as one step from the Shulcan Aruch, he found himself spiritually in the sphere of everything base" (170). His insistence on obeying not only the Bible but the Shulcan Aruch—the sixteenth-century written codification of Jewish law—testifies to a near fanatical reverence for the word that marks traditional belief.

An identical belief in the power of words animates the many diaries, journals, memoirs, and fictions that memorialize the Holocaust. Writers compulsively document the horrors they have witnessed, as though the truth of Jewish words might counter the force of German arms. Some such

mystical confidence in words is unconsciously expressed by Yadwiga, who attends Rosh Hashana
services clinging to Herman's gift of a prayer book
printed in Hebrew and English, neither of which
she can read. Understanding little Yiddish, she
nonetheless listens only to Yiddish programs on
the radio, asks Herman to speak Yiddish to her,
and tries to learn the Yiddish alphabet from an elderly Jewish immigrant. Her touching attempts to
cope with the language as well as the mores of
Jews signal an intuitive awareness of the symbolic
importance of words and prefigure her formal conversion to Judaism. Only by means of words does
Herman eke out a precarious living ghost-writing
Rabbi Lampert's speeches and articles, and later by
working briefly in Reb Abraham Nissen's bookstore. An instinctive reliance on words probably
influences his lies to Yadwiga about being a book
salesman. Since the major characters in *Enemies*
are recent immigrants, their isolation is defined in
terms of language. Speaking only Polish, Yadwiga
cannot communicate even with many Jews, let
alone Gentiles; Masha and Shifrah Puah speak
several languages, none of which does them much
good in the Bronx; Herman, fluent in Yiddish, Polish, and Hebrew, is constantly apprehensive about
his rudimentary English. In Poland, Singer's Jews
could employ language as a conscious statement of

affiliation, the ultraorthodox refusing to contaminate their Jewishness by speaking anything but Yiddish, the majority speaking at least enough Polish to communicate with Gentiles. Some of the more radically enlightened might defiantly choose to speak mostly Polish as a sign of their worldly sophistication and of their identification with the majority culture. *Enemies* is Singer's most linguistically constricted novel. Lacking a well-defined Jewish community and barely able to understand English, Yiddish speakers are far more isolated in New York than they ever were in Poland.

Linguistic isolation adds to the staggering losses suffered by Holocaust survivors. It is a constant reminder of lost family, lost friends, lost community, and of their own marginality. Herman, Tamara, Masha, and Shifrah Puah all claim that their lives effectively ended before they arrived in New York. They regard their survival as accidental and themselves as somehow superfluous. Often they pray for death and contemplate suicide. Masha's eventual suicide, after having survived the death camps, is grimly ironic but not uncommon. Like the gifted young Polish writer Tadeusz Borowski, whose stories comprise some of the most harrowing accounts of concentration camp life, and who survived both Auschwitz and Dachau only to kill himself years later, Masha had

lost the will to live. The compulsive search for instant gratification that marks her love affair with
Herman stems from their need to immerse themselves in the present as a means of forgetting the
past and warding off the future. When the future
impinges upon them and decisions must be made,
they can think only of swallowing an overdose of
sleeping pills and dying together. So meaningless
is the distinction between life and death, however,
that they cannot consciously choose one over the
other. Only in an epilogue, and then almost as an
afterthought, does Singer reveal Masha's suicide
and Herman's disappearance. That Herman simply vanishes from *Enemies* is the clinching proof of
his insubstantiality. The years spent hiding in
Yadwiga's hayloft have conditioned his later
action—or inaction—as profoundly as their concentration camp experiences have affected Masha,
Shifrah Puah, and Tamara. Just as the three
women recapitulate concentration camp life in
endless tales of Nazi atrocities, Herman relives his
three years of concealment by constantly "figuring
out the details of how to hide himself from the
Nazis here in Brooklyn" (11). Conditioned by the
dehumanizing tactics of their Nazi persecutors,
these Holocaust survivors are condemned to reenact the roles that were forced upon them. For
the remainder of their lives the women must be

witnesses, Herman a fugitive. To the sum of Holocaust losses that include family, friends, community, and language must be added the loss of personal identity.

While no one of these burdens is easy to bear, it is perhaps the loss of community that is most grievous since it epitomizes the loss of nearly everything else. The progressive weakening of *Yiddishkeit*, the cultural value system of traditional Judaism, is a recurring motif in Singer's fiction. Uprooted from the nurturing soil of the *shtetl*, its strength sapped by transplantation in the less hospitable climate of big-city ghettos, *Yiddishkeit* survives the Holocaust mostly in individual memory. *Enemies* is Singer's bleakest account of the loss of community and of the prospects for Jewish continuity. Shorn of their communal identities, individuals or couples cling pathetically to the Jewish past by fashioning miniature replicas of vanished communities. Yadwiga re-creates for Herman in Brooklyn not the Gentile village life she knew in Lipsk but the Jewish life she had observed as a servant in the house of Herman's father. In the face of Herman's indifference to religion she insists upon precise details of Jewish observance and seals her allegiance to Judaism in her formal conversion. Reb Abraham Nissen and his wife, Sheva Haddas, perpetuate the past in their East Broadway apartment. Details of appearance and dress—his full beard, sidelocks, and fringed garment; her high-collared dress and bonnet—combine with "half-curtains like those used in the old country" and smells of "fried onions, garlic, chicory, wax" to evoke prewar Jewish life in Poland. Sheva Haddas helps her husband compile "an anthology of the writings of the rabbis who had perished at the hands of the Nazis" (67), and they spend every Monday mourning "the martyrs in Europe." No matter how unforced their piety and how sincere their reverence for the past, their prodigious efforts to re-create traditional Jewish life on East Broadway want nourishment. In the absence of an authentic Jewish community in America the couple departs for Israel, where at least Reb Abraham Nissen may be buried "on the Mount of Olives, not among the shaved Jews in a New York cemetery" (244). Old and childless, bereft of community, the pious couple can transmit the carefully preserved values of *Yiddishkeit* to no one.

Even if the atomization of Jewish life in the wake of the Holocaust does not prefigure the end of Judaism itself, it raises the possibility that whatever Jewishness that survives will be radically altered. The shaved New York Jews among whom Reb Abraham Nissen disdains to be buried, the vulgar "modern Jewry" encountered by Herman and Masha in the Catskills, and, above all, Rabbi Lampert, epitomize the new Jew. Traditionally holy men and scholars, rabbis devoted themselves to studying and interpreting Torah and to transmitting Jewish values. Rabbi Lampert, who has made a fortune in real estate and whose speeches and articles are ghost-written by Herman, is the antithesis of the classic rabbi. This corrosive portrait of an American rabbi who reduces God to an afterthought evidences Singer's deepest pessimism about the future of Judaism. The symbolic failure of the American rabbinate to provide moral leadership for a reconstituted Jewish community throws Jews back on their individual resources. Masha's compulsive attachment to Shifrah Puah and to what her mother represents, from the time in a Lublin hospital when she called Shifrah Puah "back from the other world," to the moment when she refuses to leave her mother's corpse unburied, constitutes the same desire to preserve the valued past that motivates Reb Abraham Nissen and his wife. It is significant that the suicidal Masha postpones taking her own life until after her mother's death, and then does so only after specifying "a grave next to hers." That Masha chooses death with Shifrah Puah over life with Herman testifies not only to the bankruptcy of selfish hedonism but to her indissoluble bonding to the Jewishness that is its antithesis.

Lacking a community, Jews retain their faith by revivifying a vanished past. Yet without communal reinforcement will and memory cannot guarantee the survival of a people. Individual gestures such as Reb Abraham Nissen's wish to be buried on the Mount of Olives and Masha's insistence on a grave next to her mother's are limited affirmations at best, nonrepeatable and void of future application. Laden with the imagery of death, such gestures function chiefly as reminders that a viable Jewish community no longer exists. This loss of a Jewish world occasions a marked thematic shift in the two novels in which Singer confronts the Holocaust most directly. In *The Family Moskat* and again in *Enemies,* the penitential journey of the hero is either aborted or nullified by the impending or actual destruction of the Jewish community. Asa Heshel Bannet and Herman Broder recognize the futility and waste of their hedonistic lives, suffer pangs of remorse, and in moments of intense soul-searching vow to repent. Since both are scions of traditional families, they understand from the outset that repentance consists of returning to Jewishness. Still, despite the evident sincerity of their contrition they persist in ways of life which they have morally and intellectually rejected. Acts of penance, understandably difficult for such nihilists in the best of circumstances, become impossible in the absence of a Jewish community. Left to their manifestly slender personal resources, deprived of a people or a place to return to, they drift aimlessly, detesting themselves but powerless to change. The most unresolved of Singer's protagonists, Asa Heshel and Herman simply disappear.

The journeys that take them back to their God and to their people effect more than the personal salvation of Singer's penitents. Terminating in the Jewish community, penitential journeys are inspired by the belief in Judaism as a commonalty, not merely an accident of birth or a mode of worship. This insistence that the identity of the individual Jew is an aspect of Jewish corporate identity is the best hope for Jewish survival. The Midrash says that God goes halfway to meet those who return precisely because the penitent adds to the sum total of the Jewish community. But if the would-be penitent proves unwilling or unable to return, or if he lacks a community to return to, the symbolism of Jewish continuity must be vested elsewhere. Herman's disappearance confirms his inability to believe in a Jewish future. It is the inevitable conclusion to a career "based on guile. From microbe to man, life prevailed generation to generation by sneaking past the jealous powers of destruction." For Herman the "whole two thousand years of exile . . . had been one great act of smuggling" (247). Even if he correctly identifies the means of Jewish survival, Herman distances himself from its ends. Jews grow adept at modes of evasion to ensure their survival as a people. As practiced by Herman, "who no longer even had his faith in the Torah to depend on" (248), evasion is merely a strategy for dodging responsibility. His faithlessness, abundantly evident in his duplicitous personal relationships and in his deceptive ghost-writing for Rabbi Lampert, is most striking in his many outbursts against children. Herman's repudiation of children, born and unborn, is the verbal equivalent of Hitler's program of genocide, for it cancels the prospects of a Jewish future. Yet it is the same Herman, apparently indifferent to the fate of his people and fearing above all "to have his seed multiply like the sands of the sea" (248), who fathers Yadwiga's child, the symbolic hope of Jewish survival.

Yadwiga's daughter is born the "night before Shevuot," the joyous festival commemorating the giving of the Torah to Israel on Mount Sinai and the offering of the firstfruits of the wheat harvest to God. Besides its obvious promise of Jewish continuity the birth reaffirms the covenant with God that Herman had broken. Named Masha, the baby is the symbolic linchpin binding the Jewish past to the Jewish future. That Jewish hope must be vested in a child born to a convert is an irony previously employed by Singer in *The Slave*. In *Enemies* only Yadwiga is inspired by the faith that was burned out of the Jewish Holocaust survivors. And only Yadwiga, who wants "to have a Jewish child," is able to shoulder the moral burden of preserving the Jewish people. Her faith is the antithesis of Herman's faithlessness, her affirmation the antidote to his denial. Yadwiga and little Masha, along with Tamara, form the nucleus of a reborn Jewish community. Fittingly, they live in the very apartment vacated by Reb Abraham Nissen, whose bookstore devoted to Judaica Tamara maintains. Their symbolic reconstitution of the family invokes the ancient Jewish formula for survival. Only by the multiplication of such mini-communities can Jewish losses be offset and Judaism be preserved.

Shosha

Shosha, like *Enemies*, is a novel of remembrance. Yet they invoke the past by different means and for different ends. *Enemies* reveals the past through flashbacks that invariably depict the wartime suffering of Holocaust survivors. Building a montage of eyewitness accounts, Singer emphasizes the shared horror of experiences that have permanently traumatized his major characters. So crucial is remembrance in shaping the novel's texture that action and motivation are virtually indecipherable without reference to the past. In *Shosha,* however, the past is merely a backdrop for the personal reminiscences that Singer treats elsewhere as straightforward autobiography. Although it was published in English before *The Penitent, Shosha* is Singer's latest novel in point of composition. Serialized in Yiddish in the *Forward* in 1974 as *Soul Expeditions, Shosha* was published in English in 1978, nearly simultaneously with *A Young Man in Search of Love*, a volume of memoirs. *Shosha's* first-person narration and its slavish fidelity to actual events are unique among Singer's translated novels, and highlight his growing tendency to rely upon his life for his fiction. A short first chapter that telescopes the boyhood of Aaron Greidinger, Singer's alter ego, and an equally short epilogue that locates him after the Holocaust, sandwiches Aaron's account of his early life. Set in the Warsaw of the 1930s, his self-portrait of the artist as a young man draws its every detail from corresponding events in Singer's life. This deliberate blurring of the boundary between fact and fiction need not testify to a flagging of creative energy, but rather to Singer's endless compulsion, announced in the author's note to *In My Father's Court*, to call back "a life and environment that no longer exist and are unique." The invocation of the past in *Shosha* seems, therefore, not so much a means to an end as an end in itself.

Despite their different uses of the past, both *Enemies* and *Shosha* chronicle Jewish losses by stressing the proximity of the Holocaust. Hitler's extinction of Polish Jewry, a fait accompli in *Enemies*, looms on the horizon in *Shosha*. Sharing the setting of *The Family Moskat*, *Shosha* also shares its overpowering sense of doom, although the German bombs that punctuate the closing pages of *The Family Moskat* have yet to fall when the main action of *Shosha* concludes. Asa Heshel's despair in *The Family Moskat* is everywhere apparent in *Shosha* and is echoed in Aaron's "I know for sure that we will all be destroyed."[7] The Jews in Poland are trapped between Hitler and Stalin in a country where they are so hated that their Gentile neighbors "would not shed tears" at their demise: "Whoever is going to win this coming war will liquidate us" (131). Aware of their powerlessness to prevent their imminent destruction, many Polish Jews live lives of frenzied desperation, trying to jam all possible pleasure into their last days. "We all lived for the present—the whole Jewish community" (241), admits Aaron. Affluent Jews such as Haiml Chentshiner and intellectuals such as Morris Feitelzohn, who could easily leave the country, remain in Poland, deliberately blinding themselves to the future. Their self-induced paralysis ironically counterpoints the quickening pace of their daily lives, so that the major characters in *Shosha* appear to be running in place. Hedonistic theories of all sorts are cultivated to justify the unbridled pursuit of instant gratification. Feitelzohn conceives of a "play-temple of ideas" where indecisive pleasure-seekers would engage in "soul expeditions" to discover what might "amuse or inspire them most" (242). Haiml wants to pretend that every day is a holiday and should be celebrated accordingly, with festive meals and singing. His desire "to create our own calendar" (242) perfectly epitomizes the pathetic attempt by the Warsaw Jews to ignore the tragedy implicit in the real calendar.

For Aaron Greidinger sex provides the release from time that is the ultimate goal of Feitelzohn's soul expeditions and Haiml's festivities. A necessary component of all initiation stories, sex is nonetheless treated more obsessively in *Shosha* than in Singer's other novels. In this as in other respects *Shosha* resembles the appropriately titled

A Young Man in Search of Love, the autobiographical account of Singer's own initiation. Aaron's "lusting after the whole female gender" is expressed in his simultaneous affairs with several women whose originals appear in Singer's memoirs. Dora Stolnitz, for example, recalls his real-life Communist landlady-mistress in *A Young Man in Search of Love.* Even while he is still living with Dora, Aaron becomes involved with Haiml's wife, Celia, and shortly thereafter with Betty Slonim, the mistress of visiting American millionaire Sam Dreiman, and with Tekla, a Polish maid. The apparent aimlessness of Aaron's love life, like that of an earlier initiate, Asa Heshel of *The Family Moskat,* reflects not only an obsession with pleasure-taking while time remains but also a predictable reaction against his straitlaced traditional upbringing. Like the callow Singer of *A Young Man in Search of Love,* Aaron blushes and stammers constantly around women, remaining congenitally shy even as he adds to the number of his conquests. Although he is well into his thirties before the main action of *Shosha* concludes, Aaron remains the eternal adolescent, sharing this dubious distinction with Singer's former fictional womanizers such as Asa Heshel, Yasha Mazur, and Herman Broder. Lovers and friends habitually address Aaron by childish nicknames or diminutives. "He writes like a

grown-up but he's still a child," claims Celia, dub-
bing him Tsutsik, a name that sticks to Aaron
throughout the novel. To Shosha, he is forever
Arele, the little boyfriend of their childhood.

Shosha is the perfect title character for a novel
devoted to the remembrance of things past. Aaron's childhood sweetheart, she appears briefly—
but decisively—in the introductory chapter dealing
with his early years in Warsaw. Thereafter she
drops out of sight, only to reappear miraculously
unchanged many years later, when Aaron takes
Betty Slonim on a visit to his old neighborhood. In
a novel whose hero is drawn relentlessly back into
his own childhood, whose supporting cast is
largely recruited from earlier works, and whose
manifest purpose is to celebrate a vanished world,
Shosha embodies the unadulterated essence of the
past. Her symbolic importance in the life of her
creator—"She was my first love and actually these
kinds of love never die"[8]—is reaffirmed most re-
cently in "The Beginning." Shosha figures promi-
nently in this revealing piece of "spiritual
autobiography," written in 1984 to introduce the
collected edition of Singer's three volumes of
memoirs. "The Beginning" recapitulates the childhood relationship between Aaron and Shosha,
down to the very story he tells her about King Solomon's wives and treasures. She fills Aaron's

dreams as her real-life counterpart filled Singer's: "I fantasized about lying with Shosha in bed," recalls Singer some seventy years later. It is the same persistence of memory, identifying Shosha with the lost innocence of his boyhood, that explains Aaron's otherwise unfathomable decision to marry her. Almost twenty years after leaving Krochmalna Street, Aaron returns with Betty to find everything exactly as it was before: "Shosha had neither grown nor aged. . . . In her eyes was the same childish fascination I remembered from the times I told her stories" (76–77). Physically and mentally retarded, locked in perpetual childhood yet innocent and incorruptible, she is the past incarnate. Much later in the novel Betty offers Aaron a visa for America, which he refuses in order to remain with Shosha, "the only woman I can trust." While Betty accepts this cynical version of his marriage, the real truth about Shosha had already come out in the aftermath of the Krochmalna Street visit, when to Betty's "What do you see in her?" Aaron replied, "I see myself" (81). So definitively is Shosha a creature of the past that when she and Aaron flee eastward to escape the German invaders, she suddenly "sat down" on the road to Bialystok, "and a minute later she was dead" (267). Detached from the past that had sustained her, Shosha ceases to exist.

What Aaron sees in Shosha is not only his own lost innocence but a vanished way of life. Krochmalna Street, so perfectly preserved that when Aaron's mother returns to her old haunts for his wedding she remarks, "Nothing has changed," is the symbolic last bastion of traditional Jewish existence. Moishe, Aaron's younger brother and a rabbi like their father, stares incredulously at Aaron's modern appearance and dress. For Moishe and their mother time has stood still; they are less amazed by Krochmalna Street's changelessness than by Aaron's transformation. It is to the timeless world of their Jewishness that Aaron sporadically yearns to return, but of course cannot. No less than kitchen smells and memories of childhood games the appearance of his mother and brother—mirror images of Singer's own—evokes the nostalgia for the past that permeates *Shosha.* Singer's idealization of a crumbling ghetto and a retarded girl is an extreme instance of his habitual advocacy of the past at the expense of the present. As usual his enlightened Jews are neurotic and ineffectual, their lives aimless and empty. Feitelzohn's soul expeditions—the blind gropings of the faithless—and Dora's Communism—the god that failed—hopelessly counterfeit religious belief. Aaron shares with Singer's other twentieth-century heroes, and with Singer himself, the inca-

pacity to return to what he calls "real Jewishness."
Yet his decision not to abandon Shosha for Betty's
visa offer is his finest moment; it testifies to his
undying devotion, if not to the substance of belief,
then at least to its symbol.

Symbolized in his personal life by his attachment to Shosha, reverence for the past also inspires Aaron's writing. His budding literary career
in Warsaw, closely paralleling Singer's own, shares
equal billing with his sexual adventures. And just
as the past—in the person of Shosha—dominates
his private life, its very existence dominates his
writing. Aaron's devotion to the minutiae of his
early family and neighborhood life expresses his
conviction "that the aim of literature was to prevent time from vanishing" (16). Like Singer, who
endlessly mines the past for his subject matter,
Aaron conceives of Krochmalna Street as "a deep
stratum of an archaeological dig which I would
never uncover. At the same time, I recalled every
house, courtyard, cheder, Hasidic studyhouse,
store; every girl, street loafer, housewife—their
voices, gestures, manners of speaking, their pecu-
liarities" (16). Nearing the end of his life in Warsaw, taking what he knows will be his last walk
down the mean streets of the Jewish ghetto, Aaron
tries "to engrave in my memory each alley, each

building, each store, each face" (257). The net effect of his early immersion in an ancient but out-
dated tradition is, however, as inhibiting as it is
inspiring. From its first sentence, when Aaron remembers that he "was brought up on three dead
languages—Hebrew, Aramaic, and Yiddish"—
Shosha raises questions about the choice of a literary medium. For an aspiring writer of Aaron's
background, choosing the appropriate language in
which to write is as crucial as deciding what to
write about. Like the young Singer, Aaron experi-
ments with Hebrew before settling on Yiddish, unable at the outset of his career "to find a style that
might create a literary domain for myself" (14).
That the choice of Yiddish doesn't guarantee an
audience is initially apparent in Aaron's many rejected manuscripts. It grows more apparent as the
note of impending doom is sounded more and
more urgently in *Shosha*. Questions of linguistic
strategy are rendered moot by the Holocaust,
which in large part destroys the audience for both
Hebrew and Yiddish literature. Singer's post-
Holocaust certainty of the imminent destruction of
Yiddish magnifies his alter ego's need to reach an
audience. Desperation underlies Aaron's foray into
the notoriously cheap and vulgar Yiddish theater.
His many rewrites of *The Maiden of Ludmir* corre-

spond to the changing whims and fancies of Sam
Dreiman, the play's financial backer, and of Betty
Slonim, its leading lady. A hopeless tangle of artis-
tic compromises, *The Maiden of Ludmir* is never
staged. Aaron's first success in reaching a large audience comes only with his serialized biography of
Jacob Frank, the false messiah, in a Yiddish
newspaper. Inspired by its popularity, Aaron begins a new novel, which, like Singer's *Satan in Goray*, deals with the earlier "messiah," Sabbatai
Zevi, and exploits the past as a window on the
present.

Nowhere in *Shosha* is it suggested that literature, even that which commemorates the past, is
anything but a poor substitute for religion. To Celia, who worships art, Aaron cynically defines
writers as the "same kind of entertainers as magi-
cians. . . . I admire someone who can balance a
barrel on his feet more than I do a poet" (59). As-
sessing a writing career that amounts to little more
than "a membership booklet from the Writers'
Club and some worthless manuscripts," Aaron re-
viles the "meaningless literature" for which he has
exchanged "four thousand years of Jewishness"
(256). But literature, no matter what its failings, is
not the natural adversary of religion; Aaron's Jewishness was lost before his writing career began.
Singer's twentieth-century heroes—Asa Heshel

Bannet, Herman Broder, and Aaron Greidinger—
know as well as their predecessors that they can
solve the problem of how best to live simply by
reclaiming this lost Jewishness. Lacking the requi-
site faith and victimized by history, Asa Heshel
and Herman can only eddy helplessly between
tradition and modernity. It is, ironically, "meaningless literature" that saves Aaron from their fate
and gives to his life the meaning theirs lack. By
devoting himself to the task of reanimating his lost
people and their vanished world, Aaron embodies
in his work the belief he cannot share. Thirteen
years after the main action of *Shosha* concludes,
Aaron, now a famous Jewish-American writer,
runs into Haiml while visiting Israel. As they sit
together in the dark of Haiml's house, their words
fleetingly call back the ghosts of long-departed
Shosha, Celia, and Feitelzohn. In the ensuing silence Aaron hears a cricket—"the same sound that
came from the cricket that chirped in our kitchen
when I was a boy. The room filled with shadows"
(276). The cricket's chirp, the ghostly shadows—
haunting reminders of the eternal presence of the
past—are the symbolic stuff of Aaron's fictions.
They are the flickering images from a sanctified
time which it is the function of Aaron's writing—
and of *Shosha*—to fix forever in memory.

UNDERSTANDING ISAAC BASHEVIS SINGER

Notes

1. Isaac Bashevis Singer, *Enemies, a Love Story* (New York: Farrar, Straus, 1972) 30. Page references in parentheses are to this edition.

2. Singer, *Love and Exile* (Garden City, NY: Doubleday, 1984) 46.

3. Peter Gay, *Freud, Jews, and Other Germans: Masters and Victims of Modernist Culture* (New York: Oxford University Press, 1978) 165.

4. George Steiner, *Language and Silence* (New York: Atheneum, 1967) 164.

5. Terence Des Pres, *The Survivor* (New York: Oxford University Press, 1976) 175.

6. Hannah Arendt, *The Jew as Pariah: Jewish Identity and Politics in the Modern Age,* ed. Ron H. Feldman (New York: Grove, 1978) 109.

7. Singer, *Shosha* (New York: Farrar, Straus, 1978) 131. Page references in parentheses are to this edition.

8. Paul Kresh, *Isaac Bashevis Singer: The Magician of West 86th Street* (New York: Dial, 1979) 294.

CHAPTER SIX

The Short Stories

The Collected Stories (1982) crystallizes Singer's achievement.[1] In this volume are forty-seven stories selected by Singer from among the more than one hundred he has written. Spanning nearly forty years of creative activity, the selections are culled from eight separate volumes. That many stories contain some of his best writing reflects Singer's preference for the short story "because only in a short story can a writer reach perfection—more than in a novel."[2] To a modern reader—impatient with the slow pace, the digressions, and the sentimentality of a good deal of Yiddish literature—the restricted format of the short story is likewise preferable to the untrammeled freedom of the novel. Singer's perceived "modernism" and its attendant popularity stem almost exclusively from the appearance of so many of his stories in such fashionable American magazines as

The New Yorker. Yet Singer is quick to deny a greater "contemporary element" even in his most recent fiction, claiming that "some of the stories which I write today are similar to those which I wrote twenty years ago and vice versa."[3] His many years in America have left their mark solely on the surface of his fiction, leaving its essence unaltered. "A story about New York cannot be like a story about Bilgoray . . . but as far as style is concerned, I think that they are basically the same."[4] Whether or not by style he also means themes, Singer discounts time and place as ordering principles of his fiction. Early or late, Polish or American, his stories, like his novels, play variations on the overriding theme of man's relationship with God.

The more ideal this relationship, the more man bends his will to that of God. Because the quality of belief that renders such observance instinctive is found rarely in the modern world, Singer's moral archetypes are generally drawn from the Polish *shtetl.* These bearers of traditional values inhabit stories which, like themselves, embody pleas in favor of simplicity. It is chiefly through the apparent simplicity of *dos kleine menschele* (the little man), the most persistently recurring figure in Yiddish literature, that oneness with God is attained. He conspicuously lacks the education and worldly experience that in Singer's moral calculus erect barri-

ers between man and God. *Dos kleine menschele* is
the antihero of a literature which celebrates his
modest virtues: piety and endurance. Antithetical
to the Western heroic ideal, which seeks to remake
the world rather than to adjust to it, he is the logi-
cal representative of an oppressed people. So remote is the possibility that *dos kleine menschele*
could leave his mark upon the world, let alone
shake it, that he embodies collective rather than
individual values. Manifest in his ironic shrug—
the quintessential gesture of *shtetl* Jews—is the
group ethos of acceptance of the lot ordained by
God.

Gimpel, the antihero of Singer's best-known
story and the literary descendant of Sholom Aleichem's Tevye, elevates credulity to a conscious—
even sophisticated—tactic for survival. Outwardly
Gimpel is the fool of the story's title, the comic
butt of every prankster in the Frampol *shtetl*. Yet
the very ease with which he is endlessly tricked
belies his apparent foolishness. For Gimpel, at
the most critical moments of his life, invariably
chooses to be fooled, and in choosing evidences
not so much his credulity as his capacity for belief.
Much of the brilliance of "Gimpel the Fool" (1953)
stems from this complex interweaving of the real
and the willed naïveté of its hero. Gimpel, who
ostensibly believes everything he is told, knows

from the outset that he is no fool. The true fools are Gimpel's tormentors, argues the rabbi: "For he who causes his neighbor to feel shame loses Paradise himself" (4). Those who delight in victimizing Gimpel are themselves victims of their incapacity to believe with him that "everything is possible." By playing the role scripted for him by the townspeople, Gimpel hopes to do them "some good." Wise enough to play the fool, Gimpel is "duped" into marrying Elka, the town whore, who delivers a child seventeen weeks after their wedding. Not only does he accept the child as his own, but he wills himself to believe that the man he spied in bed with Elka was instead the shadow of a house beam. By denying the evidence of his eyes and recanting his accusation of infidelity against Elka, Gimpel proves himself the moral superior even of the rabbi, who advises divorce. Gimpel's recantation is a necessary condition of reconciliation; only if Elka has been unjustly accused is she worthy to live with, goes the conventional wisdom. But for Gimpel, Elka's guilt or innocence is finally irrelevant; it is enough that he misses his wife and yearns to rejoin her. His conscious decision to believe the unbelievable renews his resolution always to accept what he is told. "What's the good of *not* believing? Today it's your wife you don't believe; tomorrow it's God Himself you won't take stock in" (9). More absurd even than his misplaced faith in his wayward wife is his equation of belief in Elka with belief in God. Yet his fidelity to an imagined Elka demands that same spark of intuitive faith which flares into belief in an unseen God.

The helpless love—Saul Bellow calls it "potato love" in *Herzog*—Gimpel feels for Elka extends to all living creatures, from infants and nanny goats to the townspeople who mock him. Only once, after the dying Elka confesses her deceit, does his innate faith in the order of things momentarily waver. At the behest of "the Spirit of Evil," who invades his dreams and persuades him to revenge himself against Frampol, Gimpel urinates in the dough he will bake into the village's bread. But God saves Gimpel from throwing away "Eternal Life" in an act of petty vengeance, and in the process restores the faith that Satan tempted him to deny. Gimpel rightly senses God's presence in the shrouded Elka who appears in a dream to warn him against the deceit for which she is endlessly punished. With this fresh evidence, not only of God's existence but of His concern, the ambiguity of Gimpel's identity is definitively resolved. This ambiguity, present from the beginning of the story, is indicated in the title and the opening sentence of the Yiddish, where the epithet used is *chochem*, or "sage," which often has the ironic meaning of "fool," the sense in which it is used by Elka and the villagers.[5] But the Gimpel who buries the tainted bread and goes forth from Frampol into the world, there to grow old spinning yarns about "improbable things that could never have happened" (14), is a fool no more. By virtue of the holy simplicity that led him to apprehend God's truth beyond Frampol's lies, Gimpel the fool truly becomes Gimpel the sage.

Singer's equation of simplicity with holiness is not confined to "Gimpel the Fool." Aunt Itte Fruma, "a holy woman like one of the ancients," epitomizes the Jewish ideal in "Guests on a Winter Night" (1970). Narrated by a boy named Isaac, the story consists of little more than a series of random autobiographical snapshots until the old woman suddenly appears at the Singer flat. Soon thereafter it becomes clear that she is the living embodiment of the traditional Jewish values which Rabbi Pinhos-Mendel Singer exalts and from which his two elder children stray. The children and their mother, who at first accept the uninvited guest only grudgingly, come eventually to love and admire her. Itte Fruma's steadfast piety contrasts sharply with the inconsistent beliefs of the "enlightened" Joshua and the manic-depressive behavior of the nervous Hindele. The old woman, who has surrendered her house as dowry for a

poor couple, who gives her precious gold chain to
Hindele as an engagement present, who prays
three times a day, and who wakes in the middle of
the night to lament the destruction of the Temple
is, in Pinhos-Mendel's words, "a saint." Itte Fruma's material selflessness stems from her conviction that "one takes nothing to heaven except good
deeds" (*A Friend of Kafka and Other Stories* 32). The
throng that attends her funeral belies her short residence in Warsaw and testifies to her symbolic
value for the Jewish community.

That the life of a Gimpel or an Itte Fruma mer-
its a seat in paradise is strongly implied in the endings of their stories. "Short Friday" (1964) makes
explicit the reward awaiting those who lead lives of
simple piety in accordance with God's laws.
Shmul-Leibele—small, clumsy, sterile, so ineffectual that he had never mastered his tailor's craft—
is, like Gimpel, the butt of everyone's jokes. A
pauper, he is nonetheless honest and good-
hearted, never cheating a customer and presenting
gifts of candy and nuts to the town wags who torment him. Shoshe, his beautiful and competent
wife, without whom he "would certainly have
starved to death," is the reward for his piety and
good-heartedness. Their outward poverty belies
the richness of inner lives devoted to love of God
and each other. Together they adhere faithfully to

every detail of Jewish law, taking their greatest joy in observing the Sabbath. So happy is the marriage of Shmul-Leibele and Shoshe that their only fear is that one will outlive the other, leaving the survivor broken-hearted. The ending of the story draws into a symbolic action their mutual love and fear of loss with their devotion to God. Their particular reverence for the Sabbath—the day dedicated to God—epitomizes the primacy of belief in their lives. Simultaneous death, the reward for their righteousness, comes as a natural culmination of their Sabbath feasting, drinking, and lovemaking. Serenely awaiting the Angel of Death, their escort to paradise, Shmul-Leibele recalls the identical biblical verse that sanctifies the burial of Jacob and Sarah in *The Slave:* "Lovely and pleasant in their lives, and in their death they were not divided." That their shortest Friday marks the end of natural life and the beginning of eternal life is the fitting outcome of the holy couple's last Sabbath. Ordained by God and conferred on His day, their fate is intertwined with the symbolic meaning of Sabbath and conforms to the ideal pattern of Jewish life.

To an even greater extent than in "Guests on a Winter Night" or "Short Friday," Singer identifies simple piety with the survival of traditional values and therefore of Judaism itself in "The Old Man"

(1957) and "The Little Shoemakers" (1954). Both stories are overtly allegorical accounts of miraculous rejuvenation. At their centers are Jewish patriarchs whose journeys and rebirths resonate with the promise of Jewish continuity. Reb Moshe Ber, the old man of his story's title, and Abba Shuster, the paterfamilias of "The Little Shoemakers," are explicitly compared to Abraham, the patriarch of the Jewish people. To underline the drama of Jewish survival played out by his ancient protagonists, Singer locates them amidst the greatest cataclysms of modern history—the two world wars. Two years after he had uprooted himself from Jozefow to live with his prosperous son in Warsaw, the ninety-year-old Reb Moshe Ber finds himself suddenly alone and starving, the sole family survivor of the Great War. For weeks he drags himself, more dead than alive, south through war-ravaged Poland, to arrive in Jozefow just in time to spend Yom Kippur with his fellow Hasidim. Although the arduous journey on the part of an ill and starving non-agenerian—who incidentally refuses to eat any but kosher food en route—is a sufficiently miraculous allegory of Jewish survival, still greater wonders animate the story's climax. The birth of a son named Isaac to a deaf and dumb spinster of forty exactly nine months after her wedding to Reb Moshe Ber simultaneously certifies the old man's righteousness and promises his people's survival. Sealing his identification with Abraham as patriarch of the Jews, the miraculous birth restores to Reb Moshe Ber the son who will one day say Kaddish over his grave. Such is the old man's reward for the simple faith—"God will help me"—that inspired his will to live, that sustained him through his harrowing journey, and that vested in him the hope for Jewish survival.

The same invincible will, again manifest in a journey which ends in personal and familial renewal, characterizes Abba Shuster in "The Little Shoemakers." Singer's story spans the entirety of modern Jewish history from "some time after Chmielnitzki's pogroms" when the first Abba Shuster appeared in Frampol until shortly after the outbreak of World War II when his great-great-grandson, the last Abba Shuster, boards "the last ship for the United States" and rejoins his seven sons in a New Jersey suburb. Abba's archetypal identity stretches, however, far beyond the three hundred years of his family's existence in Frampol: "When his wife, Pesha, read to him, of a Sabbath, from the Yiddish translation of the stories in the Book of Genesis, he would imagine that he was Noah, and that his sons were Shem, Ham, and Japheth. Or else he would see himself in the image of Abraham, Isaac, or Jacob" (40). Throughout the

THE SHORT STORIES

story, culminating in a stormy Atlantic crossing during which he likens himself to Jonah in the belly of the whale, Abba habitually stresses the seamless continuity of Jewish history—"as if he too were part of the Bible" (40). In his fascination with biblical lore and identification with biblical patriarchs Abba embodies the persistence of a Jewish tradition outwardly symbolized by the ruined house in which generations of his family had lived and died. Abba cannot bring himself to tear down this wreck, whose walls were family albums and whose shadows concealed the souls of ever-watchful forefathers. To the simple and pious Abba, for whom change is anathema, his seven sons' one-by-one desertion of Frampol for America is inconceivable. Resisting their sons' pleas, he and Pesha remain in Frampol wrapped in the timeless skein of traditional *shtetl* life. For more than forty years, and long after Pesha's death, Abba clings to the only way of life he can imagine. Only the German bombs that fell on Frampol, destroying his house and driving him into the archetypal night of Jewish exile, finally dislodge him from his traditional moorings. Uprooted from his timeless *shtetl* home, Abba is thrust by history into the terrifying role of the homeless refugee. Like Reb Moshe Ber's hazardous trek from Warsaw to Jozefow, Abba's flight through Romania, thence by

train to Italy, and finally by ship to America recapitulates the suffering of the Jewish exile. The possibility that Jewish tradition has suffered a fatal
blow, symbolically raised by the destruction of Abba's house, is intensified by the loss of his phylacteries and prayer shawl. Unlike Reb Moshe Ber,
whose revitalization occurs automatically when he
reaches Jozefow, Abba finds himself in a world
conspicuously devoid of Jewish communal havens.
Safe at last in New Jersey but bereft of the community that nurtured Reb Moshe Ber, Abba suffers
from "disordered" senses and "constant anxiety."
Only when he finds his shoemaker's tools from
Frampol and again practices his trade does Abba
seem fifteen years younger and take on "new life."
The shoemaker's craft, plied by every male Shuster
(the name means "shoemaker") for the past three
hundred years, provides the crucial link to tradition without which Abba would wither and die.
When his sons join him at the workbench, their
solidarity is not merely nostalgic. Rather it reveals
the enduring power of the Jewish tradition and
how that tradition may be preserved in America.
That his sons fall so happily to work is taken by
Abba for a sign: "They had not forgotten their heritage" (56). Together they attain a collective Jewish
identity which inspires hope that Jewish commu-

nal life, wiped out in Europe, may be miraculously restored in America.

The richly affirmative endings of "The Old Man" and "The Little Shoemakers" derive from the steadfast faith of their central characters. Because the simple piety of a Moshe Ber or an Abba Shuster expresses itself in unquestioning acceptance of what God ordains, the proper relationship between man and God is maintained. In equally affirmative stories, however, the equilibrium of this relationship is temporarily disrupted. A momentary lapse of faith or a sin once committed and never repeated may drive a wedge between man and God that must, in the course of the story, be removed. "Joy" (1957) depicts the crisis of faith that overcomes Rabbi Bainish of Komarov, who, having buried his four sons and two daughters, cries, "There is no justice, no Judge" (31). Only through the mercy of the God he denied, manifest in a radiant vision of the dead Rebecca, his beloved youngest daughter, is the rabbi's belief restored. The "sense of wonder" and the "touch of heavenly joy" that linger after the vision dissolves convince Rabbi Bainish of the folly of judging God's actions by human standards. The rabbi had interpreted the apparent tragedy of his children's premature deaths as evidence of God's alienation, forgetting that God is by definition inscrutable. That God's purpose transcends man's ability to comprehend it is made clear to the expiring rabbi when the family dead approach his deathbed with arms outstretched to enfold him among them. For theirs is the kingdom of heaven to which a loving God has called them; and their early deaths evidenced not God's wrath but His grace.

A version of Rabbi Bainish's deathbed revelation appears to Rabbi Nechemia in "Something Is There" (1970). At twenty-seven he is already racked by the doubts that torment Rabbi Bainish. So shaken is his belief in God that he deserts his rabbinical post in provincial Bechev for the fleshpots of Warsaw. Although the prostitutes, unclean food, and shady business dealings which he witnesses there hold no attraction for the erstwhile rabbi, they intensify his revulsion from the world created by God and therefore his alienation from God himself. Unlike Rabbi Bainish, whose intimations of immortality and consequent rededication to God precede his radiant deathbed vision, Rabbi Nechemia cannot allay his doubts until the very moment of death, when "a light he never knew was there flickered in his brain" (350). While his dying words—"Something is there"—resolve his crisis of faith, they come too late to effect the spiritual renewal attained by Rabbi Bainish. No explicit promise of immortality, let alone of salvation, attends Rabbi Nechemia's vision. Perhaps grace is accorded Rabbi Bainish because his doubt is triggered by devastating personal losses, and withheld from Rabbi Nechemia because his despair is the bitter fruit of idle speculation about the unkown. Whatever the reason, relatively few of Singer's characters are granted at the moment of death the transcendent vision of unity between man and God that appears to the couple in "Short Friday" and to Rabbi Bainish in "Joy." For the fortunate few, release from time into eternity is effected by a divine visitation which obliterates distinctions between past and present, living and dead.

Nowhere in Singer's fiction is this united vision more pervasive and more all-encompassing than it is in "A Wedding in Brownsville" (1964). As in the ending of *The Slave*, when Jacob is buried next to Sarah amidst the Jewish dead in the Pilitz cemetery, "A Wedding in Brownsville" celebrates the eternal oneness of the Jewish people. Dr. Solomon Margolin, the hero of "A Wedding in Brownsville," seems an unlikely candidate for grace. An atheist whose hope for the future and faith in humanity had been destroyed along with his family by the Germans, Margolin is an aging philanderer married to a Gentile wife. Still, he is devoted to the Jewish community and to his profession, and

"his sense of honor amounted to a mania." Like
Ezriel Babad, the enlightened physician of *The Manor* and *The Estate*, Dr. Margolin is redeemed not
by his piety but by his works. Especially in the
post-Holocaust era, Singer reckons moral worth by
standards different from those applied to Jews living in more or less intact and traditional prewar
communities. Simple decency now suffices in lieu
of strict adherence to Jewish law; in the wake of
the Holocaust it is enough to have been a victim
rather than a victimizer. By centering his drama of
communal salvation around Dr. Margolin, a good
man despite his skepticism and restlessness,
Singer implies that in the debased modern world
one is hard pressed to find a better representative
Jew. So it is Margolin whose taxi ride through a
surreal landscape enveloped in snow becomes the
first stage of a symbolic passage from life through
death to union with the spiritual community. "In
this literal modern elaboration of the *Zohar's* stories of good men escorted through death to paradise by their dead families, Dr. Margolin's
consciousness carries him from his fatal accident to
the wedding."[6] At the spectral wedding, an extended epiphany climaxed by the appearance of
Raizel, Dr. Margolin's long-dead first love, the
lines between past and present, youth and age, life
and death, melt away. Because the wedding re-

unites him not only with Raizel but with the destroyed Sencimin community, Dr. Margolin's epiphany transcends even Rabbi Bainish's in "Joy."

The lesson learned by Rabbi Bainish is a corollary to the one implied in Singer's tales of simple piety. Gimpel, Reb Moshe Ber, and Abba Shuster waste no time thinking about belief; they simply act. By agonizing over the nature and purposes of God, Rabbi Bainish succeeded only in reasoning himself into despair. Theorizing about faith is not only futile but unnecessary, since even an unbeliever can, by sheer force of will, approximate the life of the pious. Too much thought undermines the belief of Asa Heshel (*The Family Moskat*) and Herman Broder (*Enemies*), while Ezra Babad (*The Estate*) and Joseph Shapiro (*The Penitent*) come to understand that if they act as though they believed, faith will someday follow. In the aptly titled "A Piece of Advice" (1961) the holy Rabbi Chazkele urges a congenitally angry man to avoid doing wrong merely by doing right, thereby turning "the worst sin into a good deed. The main thing is to act, not to ponder" (*The Spinoza of Market Street* 144). Indeed, the sinner's conversion is ennobled by the great effort it costs him. After Rabbi Chazkele's death the formerly angry man, now "so good-natured it was unbelievable," attracts disciples of his own whom he in turn advises: "If you can't be a good Jew, act the good Jew, because if you act something, you *are* it" (144).

A variation on this theme occurs in "A Nest Egg for Paradise" (1985) when the pious Reb Mendel succumbs to his sexy sister-in-law "in an instant of sheer drunkenness and utter helplessness." Although this sin is the sole blemish on an otherwise untainted life, Reb Mendel believes it has cost him "the world to come." Dwelling on his depravity, he prays for death to atone for his sinfulness. It is this very certainty of his own iniquity and of its inevitable consequences which, more than his brief spasm of lust, threatens his spiritual well-being. For Reb Mendel's most grievous failing is his inability to apprehend God's infinite mercy, by virtue of which even the most heinous sin may be forgiven. Crippled by a form of intellectual pride that causes him to usurp God's role by prejudging himself, he never regains confidence in his ultimate salvation. Only when Reb Mendel ceases brooding about the world to come and dedicates himself to the service of God "without expecting any rewards" does he find peace.

A more radical theory of justification through deeds, again a by-product of Singer's habitual plea for simplicity, emerges from "I Place My Reliance on No Man" (1961). Endlessly plagued by complaints from the people he so piously and unselfishly serves, Rabbi Jonathan Danziger is driven sometimes "to question the ways of God and even doubt His mercy" (*Short Friday and Other Stories* 210). Little by little it occurs to the rabbi that his enemies "were either the rich or the lazy idlers." It is this insight that inspires him to take the extraordinary step of resigning his post to pick fruit in Shloime Meyer's orchard. By casting his lot with honest workers who represent the simple Jewish values that the religious politics of his tormentors distorted, Danziger achieves spiritual renewal. That to do so he must forsake the rabbinate, in which spiritual values are traditionally vested, is an ironic but apparently necessary prelude to the peace he seeks. The ending of this puzzling story seems to suggest that if one cannot serve God and man at the same time, he is better off choosing one or the other. Some such conclusion influenced Ezriel Babad's decision near the end of *The Estate* to resume his medical practice in Israel. Unable to dedicate himself to God, he is redeemed through his service to man.

Since few possess the instinctive and wholehearted belief in God that sustains Gimpel or the couple in "Short Friday," skeptics are more the rule than the exception in Singer's fiction. Their stories generate tension from the interplay between faith and doubt that is missing from stories whose protagonists are unfailingly holy. This tension is resolved in sudden flashes of insight which reveal the presence of a higher power. As a direct result of the knowledge thus acquired, a more or less profound change occurs, if not of habit, then at least of mind. Two revelations modify the hero's self-image and thereby determine the outcome of "Alone" (1962). Set in contemporary Miami Beach, the story grows progressively surreal in ironic response to its hero's wish to be alone. Because the first-person narration is retrospective, a crucial aspect of the story is revealed at the outset in the narrator's realization that "Hidden Powers" granted his wish in order "to show me I didn't understand my own needs" (140). Ostensibly a reaction to being fed up with the tourist scene, the narrator's wish actually masks his desire for sexual adventure. The sudden closing of his hotel, occasioning his move to an empty run-down fleabag presided over by a hunchbacked Cuban girl "with black piercing eyes," represents the melting away of social restraints. Granted the license he has subconsciously sought, he dreams of a "hot-eyed woman" moving into the hotel, at the same time chiding the imp who, perhaps deliberately, took his wish to be alone too literally. By the imp the narrator means the "Hidden Powers," which have provided him with an empty hotel but which might just as easily have undone him. As though to confirm his intuition that "some kind of superior being has to be hidden in back of all these illusions" (142) a storm of apocalyptic intensity breaks out. The storm transforms Miami Beach into a surreal landscape of monstrous billows, somersaulting chairs, and careening signs. Analogous to the distortions produced in nature is the half-dissolved image of the narrator reflected in his mirror "like a figure in a cubist painting." At the height of the storm the Cuban hunchback materializes in the "hellish glare of walls turned scarlet," ironically fulfilling his dream of a woman who would come to him in an empty hotel. The Satanic imagery that surrounds and defines her—only snout and tail are missing—comprises an epiphany of evil and a warning against it. Invoking the name of God to ward off her sexual advances, the narrator rejects the sinfulness she represents. To the girl his refusal is hypocritical, the product of physical revulsion rather than of faith in God. Whether she is correct is, however, irrelevant in Singer's moral calculus. No matter what his motivation, the narrator has consciously chosen good over evil. His decision, triggered by the apparition that God had mercifully called up to deflect him from evil, admits the existence of the demonic forces with which he has dangerously toyed and sets him back on the path of righteousness.

Less startling are the means of provoking a change of heart in two aging and lonely people, Bessie Popkin ("The Key," 1970) and Herman Gombiner ("The Letter Writer," 1968). Bessie, a childless widow whose husband, Sam, has been dead for twenty years, leads the life of a recluse in her New York apartment, seldom straying more than two blocks from the building. Her total alienation from people stems from paranoid fear of their intentions. To Bessie the Puerto Rican milkman is a potential rapist, her neighbors are prospective thieves, and the building superintendent is a conspirator with orders to evict her from her rent-controlled apartment by infesting it with rats, mice, and cockroaches. It is the apparently trivial incident of a broken key that initiates a series of minor epiphanies culminating in the major revelation of the story's climax. At first Bessie's paranoia intensifies to the point of conceiving the loss of the key as a punishment sent by God. Yet her increasing hysteria, symptomized by her sudden outburst in Yiddish, is employed by Singer to reawaken Bessie's lost humanity. Her cry in the "half-forgotten tongue" of her youth releases the pent-up feelings—for God, for Sam and the souls of her parents, even for a cat that rubs against her—that in her selfish and suspicious isolation Bessie had long suppressed. As if scales had dropped from her eyes, she is now able to perceive the superintendent as helpful, the neighbors as solicitous, and even passersby as friendly. At this point, her symbolic resurrection attained, another writer might end Bessie's story. But for Singer the full meaning of "The Key" lies in the transcendent revelation which her conversion prefigures. The story's final paragraph makes it clear that Bessie's reconciliation to life is the necessary prelude to the vision that attends her death. That Sam's appearance is contingent upon her change of heart is apparent in the words he once spoke on the first night of their honeymoon and which he speaks again at heaven's gate: "You don't need no key here. Just enter—and *mazel tov*" (*A Friend of Kafka and Other Stories* 49). In congratulating Bessie for gaining paradise, her husband congratulates the bride she has again become in order to merit salvation.

A different form of salvation comes to Herman Gombiner, "a bachelor, almost fifty years old, and a sick man" (250), the title character of "The Letter Writer." Like so many of Singer's Jewish refugees who have lost their families in the Holocaust, Herman is prematurely aged, physically decrepit, and alone in New York. In his name, his appearance, his vegetarianism, his concern for animals, his aversion to children, and his reliance on Judaica for work, he is an earlier version of Herman Broder (*Enemies*). Whereas Broder compensates for his losses by movement and mistresses, Gombiner takes refuge in stasis and isolation. Both truncated life styles are no more fully human than Bessie's in "The Key." Herman Broder is beyond help; but Herman Gombiner is rescued by a miraculous intervention. Until the timely appearance of Rose Beechman—attributed to her clairvoyance, but properly read as a miracle sent by God—Herman drifts downward into death. Endlessly falling snow—a favorite Singer symbol for impending death—attends Herman's willing surrender to oblivion after he loses his job. Herman, whose "real sustenance was the letters he received," and whose closest living friend is the mouse he names Huldah, lives most truly in sleep, the bringer of dreams but also the harbinger of death. He shares with his correspondents an interest in the occult, considering himself among "the select few privileged to see beyond the façade of phenomena" (251). As elsewhere in Singer, such belief in the supernatural is tantamount to belief in God, who manifests Himself through "the apparitions, telepathic incidents, clairvoyant visions, and prophetic dreams" (253) that Herman claims to have experienced. What Herman requires is not an infusion of belief but evidence that life is precious and more than the "eternal Treblinka" he imagines. Rose Beechman's arrival two weeks earlier than expected, ostensibly at the behest of her dead grandmother, links clairvoyance with the faith in God that lies behind it. Though not even a Jewess, Rose becomes a ministering angel sent by God in Herman's hour of greatest need. Yet even as he acknowledges that God has brought him back to life, Herman resents His having done so. At some risk of trivializing Herman's epiphany, Singer insists upon juxtaposing the sudden surge of love for Rose with love for a mouse. For it is the appearance of Huldah, given up for dead, that provides Herman with the clinching evidence of "pure grace" which he needs in order to prefer life to death. Huldah's miraculous survival transcends bathos to become proof of the reverence for all things both great and small that inspires God's mercy. The same reverence for "all God's creatures" inspires Rose to bear the burden of nursing Herman back to health. At the end of the story the falling snow—"a dawn snow"—signals not the onset of death but of rebirth. Night ends and day breaks with the cries of children, the shrieks of housewives, and the blaring of radios—life. "It all had," for Herman, "the quality of a revelation" (276).

A similar promise of salvation through love is held out to the very dissimilar protagonists of "The Spinoza of Market Street" (1961) and "The Shadow of a Crib" (1961). At first glance the ailing and elderly Jewish scholar, Dr. Fischelson, and the lusty and dynamic Gentile physician, Dr. Yaretzky, have little in common. Both, however, are disciples of philosophers who fascinated the young Singer and bewitched several of his most important characters. Like Asa Heshel Bannet (*The Family Moskat*), Dr. Fischelson goes nowhere without his volume of Spinoza, even poring over the *Ethics* while waiting to be served in the market. And the atheist Dr. Yaretzky relies upon Schopenhauer to buttress his morbid view of human nature and his nihilistic model of the world. Both men suffer from the same symptoms that afflict so many of Singer's disaffected intellectuals and arise from their penchant for distorting life by forcing it into the straitjacket of unyielding dogma. In each case love appears, to call philosophy into doubt. Faced with conflict between their emotional instincts and their entrenched habits of thought, the two follow divergent paths. No matter that Dr. Fischelson's surrender to love may be rooted in age and infirmity or may prove impermanent, Singer makes it clear that his ability to extricate himself, however fleetingly, from Spinoza constitutes an affirmation of life diametrically opposed to the rejection Dr. Yaretzky effects by failing to dislodge Schopenhauer.

After thirty years of studying Spinoza's *Ethics*, Dr. Nahum Fischelson's thought is nearly indistinguishable from that of the philosopher he reveres. Since Spinoza distrusted emotions and stressed independence, Dr. Fischelson has never married and deplores the passionate rabble whose behavior is "the very antithesis of reason" (82). Although his late father was the rabbi of Tishevitz, Dr. Fischelson has alienated himself from the Jewish community, which views Spinoza's teachings as heretical. Another of Singer's flawed scholarly Jews, Dr. Fischelson has lost a promising career and the better part of his life in his single-minded devotion to a philosophical system that promises harmony but delivers only loneliness. When in 1914 the meager pension from Berlin that provides his livelihood is cut off by the outbreak of World War I, Dr. Fischelson thinks momentarily of suicide until he remembers "that Spinoza did not approve of suicide" (85). The instantaneous collapse of his insular world in the face of external reality is indicative of its fragility and of the shortcomings of its philosophical rationale. Only the fortuitous appearance of the swarthy and illiterate Black Dobbe, one of the unreasoning rabble for whom Dr. Fischelson has so much contempt, saves him from death. That his health, rapidly declining under Spinoza's hard tutelage, improves so dramatically under Dobbe's tender ministrations proves that cold reason cannot take the place of human warmth. And by marrying Black Dobbe in a traditional Jewish ceremony, Dr. Fischelson gains not only a wife but a people: "We are all brethren now" (91). But the greatest miracle is reserved for their wedding night, when the aged and infirm scholar whose trembling hand could barely slip the ring on his wife's finger and whose foot is too weak to shatter the goblet, becomes "again a man as in his youth." As Dobbe embraces him, Spinoza's *Ethics* falls from his hands, and Dr. Fischelson achieves union with her and with humanity. With love comes surcease of physical pain and remembrance of romantic poetry, and finally the "deep sleep young men know." Waking to gaze from his open window into Spinoza's illimitable space amidst which a single marriage is infinitesimal, Dr. Fischelson murmurs, "Divine Spinoza, forgive me. I have become a fool" (93). The apology is as ironic as it is pathetic, for it is Spinoza who has so long betrayed Dr. Fischelson; and only by betraying Spinoza this one time can Dr. Fischelson reclaim the life that philosophy has cost him. Becoming a fool is tantamount to living, since only by mindlessly accepting the divine miracle that philosophy cannot explain can a Dr. Fischelson be restored and the duality between thought and feeling be resolved.

To be a candidate for redemption a Singer character must either believe in God or retain the capacity to do so. Although Dr. Fischelson's belief that God is everywhere and that everyone is a part of God owes itself to Spinoza rather than to Jewish dogma, he never denies God's existence. And certain aspects of Spinoza's philosophy—the idea that morality and happiness are identical, for example—actually reinforce or parallel Jewish belief. To Dobbe's inquiry he replies, "Yes, I believe," and he weds her in a traditional Jewish ceremony conducted "according to the law." Dr. Yaretzky's claim that "there is no God" would seem to disqualify him for redemption in "The Shadow of a Crib." Here, as elsewhere, however, Singer makes the point that God is merciful: "He has compassion even for those who profane Him" (*The Spinoza of Market Street* 65) As if to confirm God's grace, Yaretzky is offered a second chance to marry Helena, his potential savior from a life of moral cynicism and spiritual negation. The first of her two kisses convinces him of her love but not of any desire on his part to marry, since he shares Schopenhauer's view of women as no more than a "vessel of sex, which blind will has formed for its own purposes—to perpetuate the eternal suffering and tedium" (82). Yet Helena's kiss has shaken Yaretzky's philosophical certitude sufficiently for him to entertain the notion of a seeing universe rather than a blind one. After leaving the ball, he wanders past the house of the town's pious rabbi and glimpses the rabbi's wife rousing herself in the middle of the night to attend to her husband's samovar. While Yaretzky falls short of interpreting this moment—and every moment—as preordained by God, he is impressed by the deep faith that underlies the "love ritual" he has witnessed. This instance of selfless fidelity belies Schopenhauer's dim view of women and lets Yaretzky imagine a scheme of things in which Helena's kiss expresses not the blind will of a predatory female but the all-seeing will of God. Shortly thereafter, Yaretzky's apparently aimless wanderings take him down the path toward Helena's estate: "His feet seemed to have brought him here of their own volition. . . . He was searching for something, he did not know what" (80). That something turns out to be Helena, who has swallowed poison, and who averts death solely by virtue of Yaretzky's timely intervention. For the second time that day Helena

kisses his hand; and this time the formerly dis-
dainful doctor returns her kiss. In his kiss and subsequent marriage proposal Yaretzky seems tacitly
to acknowledge the power beyond sheer chance
that led him from the ball past the rabbi's window
to Helena's side. The episode has all the earmarks
of the second chance proffered by God in so many
stories and prefigured near the beginning of "The
Shadow of a Crib."

Yaretzky's tragedy—and Helena's—stems from
his failure to translate his momentary brush with
grace into a permanent change of heart. His flight
and Helena's subsequent retreat into a convent
represent the triumph of despair over hope. Like
so many of Singer's intellectuals Dr. Yaretzky becomes the victim of his own thought process; released for a brief moment from Schopenhauer's
nihilism, he has "reasoned" his way back to it.
The part of himself that sought to embrace life has
been ruthlessly suppressed by the greater part that
has habitually denied love. Dr. Yaretzky saves Helena's life only to annul it; denied the love which
alone can make her whole, she withers away in
her convent. When, many years later, Yaretzky's
ghost haunts the crumbling estate where Helena
once had lived, women swear that her voice is
heard crooning lullabies as to an infant, and that
on the wall of her former room appears the

shadow of a crib. Yaretzky's unquiet soul and Helena's spectral song testify to the unfulfilled potential of their love, symbolized by the unborn child and the empty crib.

While Dr. Fischelson's years of solitude and Dr. Yaretzky's lost love are the sad wages of intellectual pride, Singer's most severe punishments are reserved for those who commit graver sins of the intellect. Like Faustus, the literary archetype of intellectual pride, who knows so much yet so little, they are undone by the very thought that nurtured them. These wholly reckless and self-seeking pursuers of knowledge distort or abrogate their belief in God and become the unwitting tools and allies of Satan, who narrates their stories. Satan's ironic commentary counterpoints the action of "Zeidlus the Pope" (1943, 1964) and "The Destruction of Kreshev" (1943, 1961), interpreting it in a light that dawns on the intellectually proud only when it is too late to save themselves. The endings of these and similar stories narrated by Satan make it clear that they have been scripted by the archfiend and not by their deluded protagonists. Tricked into making common cause against God, prideful intellectuals are momentarily sustained by Satan only to be relentlessly destroyed by their erstwhile ally. Zeidel Cohen, whose sole weakness is "more than that sliver of vanity which the Law permits the scholar," is tempted by the Evil One to convert, since the "Chosen People hate greatness" (172). So consuming is Zeidel's desire that his erudition be honored that he forgets that Jews refuse to honor man because greatness is solely an attribute of God. The same misplaced intellectual pride that drives Zeidel to pay the price of apostasy for greatness lies at the root of his failure to gain what he so single-mindedly desires. Hoping like former converts to achieve instant fame by writing anti-Jewish polemics, the would-be pope begins one of those interminable philosophical treatises that in Singer's fiction signify intellectual confusion rather than accomplishment. Led by his own impossibly high standards into more and more obscure scholarly byways, Zeidel ends by doubting all faiths, his *Apologia Contra Talmudum* never completed. Afflicted by blindness and pain, the man who would be pope grows old as a mendicant. No longer plagued by earthly desires, he still yearns to know "the truth." Only when Satan comes for him does that truth become apparent to Zeidel: "If Hell exists, everything exists. If you are real, He is real" (178). That Zeidel must pay the price of his immortal soul for the wisdom possessed by the most ignorant Jew is poetic justice for the proud intellectual who betrayed his God and wasted his life in striving to learn what he should have known all along. A powerful plea for simplicity as well as an indictment of worldly ambition and perverted learning, "Zeidlus the Pope" raises the stakes of "The Spinoza of Market Street" and "The Shadow of a Crib." Misplaced faith, no longer embodied in isolation or unrequited love but in apostasy, now risks everlasting damnation.

Even a little learning of the wrong sort may endanger one's immortal soul. The intellectual restlessness which prompts Akhsa to rummage through her dead grandfather's library shatters her life in "A Crown of Feathers" (1973). It is her learning, which has already set her apart from other Jewish girls, that enables Akhsa to read a Polish translation of a "forbidden" book: the New Testament. Such reading may lead to no grave immediate consequences for Singer's Jews, but it is often the first symptom of waywardness. Addicted to the romantic novels that promise relief from the constraints of a traditional Jewish upbringing, Miriam Lieba (*The Manor*) opts for the "freedom" that destroys her. Sharing Miriam Lieba's volatile mix of beauty and brains, Akhsa also shares her fate— apostasy. Both refuse arranged matches with pious and scholarly though physically unprepossessing Jewish youths to marry dissolute Polish aristocrats. In "A Crown of Feathers" piety and apostasy, personified respectively by the ghostly voices of her grandfather and grandmother, vie for Akhsa's soul. The triumph of evil is the end product of the intellectual arrogance that causes Akhsa to value her own judgment above her grandfather's, driving Zemach away and hastening the old man's death. The same pride of intellect that opened Zeidel to Satan's temptations blinds Akhsa to the Devil's handiwork. Confident of her ability to read the signs around her, Akhsa takes the crown of feathers as evidence of the truth of Christianity and converts.

Years later, her marriage in shambles, her belief lost, Akhsa comes to recognize the Devil's role in fashioning the crown of feathers and persuading her to convert. Just as pride led her to err, humility—signaled by her prayer "to the God she had forsaken" and the spectral appearance of the grandfather she had betrayed—leads her to repent. Akhsa's return—to Zemach and to Jewishness—traces the familiar arc described by Singer's penitents. Yet questions about the nature of truth persist. Akhsa finds Zemach an ascetic sadomasochist, bent on harsh retribution and violent self-mortification. Although he claims that his abuse springs from love and the wish to "cleanse" her, its effect is to validate Akhsa's original decision not to marry him. Never does Akhsa fully embrace the Devil's position: "The truth is that there is no truth" (371). But neither does she attain the peace which her hard penance seems to merit. On her deathbed she again spies the crown of feathers, once indicative of the truth of Christianity, now apparently proof of the efficacy of Judaism; once the Devil's doing, now apparently God's artifact. The crown's ambiguous symbolism points to the elusiveness of truth: If truth exists, "it is as intricate and hidden as a crown of feathers" (371). More than a disquisition on the relativity of truth, however, "A Crown of Feathers" is a cautionary tale about the dangers of forbidden knowledge. Only by straying from the path of traditional Jewish life does Akhsa wander into the swamp of religious and philosophical relativism. The story's indecisive conclusion mirrors her doubt, which, once awakened, cannot be quelled even by the most rigorous penance. And the unquiet state of Akhsa's soul owes itself to that fatal moment in her grandfather's library when she first opened the New Testament.

One needn't be an intellectual to risk damnation. In "Blood" (1964) the passion for blood and the passion for flesh are united in Risha, the personification of lust. Like Zeidel, the personification of pride, she converts to Christianity and is eventually punished by Satan. Transformed into a werewolf, the epitome of her animalistic nature,

Risha is first axed to death by the men whose community she has defiled, then thrown into an unmarked ditch, and finally roasted in hell. Yet despite the communal involvement in her fate Risha's sins, like Zeidel's, affect only the individual sinner. When intellectual pride takes the form of sexual depravity in "The Destruction of Kreshev," fire and plague destroy an entire town and its inhabitants. Although corruption is confined to the unholy *ménage à trois* of Shloimele, Lise, and Mendel, their sins are so grave as to liken Kreshev to Sodom and Gomorrah, with analogous results. Each of the three sexual miscreants epitomizes an aspect of deviant behavior which leads inevitably to disaster in Singer's fiction. As in "Blood," sexual depravity is the outward symptom of moral depravity. Governed by their several impulses to free themselves from traditional restraints, the three sinners end by so distorting prescribed human relationships as to call down God's wrath upon Kreshev. Shloimele, a yeshiva prodigy, is a secret follower of Sabbatai Zevi, the false messiah. Like certain Zevi adherents of *Satan in Goray,* Shloimele would hasten the end of days by acts of defilement, since the Messiah will come only when a generation is either totally pure or totally impure. It is his conviction that total impurity is the more likely scenario that prompts him to talk Lise into sleeping with Mendel, the sin which triggers the conflagration he so desires: "I love fire! I love a holocaust . . . I would like the whole world to burn and Asmodeus to take over the rule" (115). Shloimele's intellectual pride finds its counterpart in Lise, who marries him for his prodigious learning despite his unprepossessing looks. In Lise's love of learning lie the seeds of her undoing, for her intense interest in books, evidenced at an early age, is regarded as unnatural by Singer's traditional Jews and severely compromises her femininity. Her tragedy is prefigured in her father's warning that studying is no preparation for marriage—a woman's only legitimate career—and in his wistful regret that she hadn't been born a boy: "What a man she would have made" (98). Like Hindele, who gives birth to a devil in "The Black Wedding," (1961), and Yentl, who marries another woman in "Yentl the Yeshiva Boy" (1962), Lise distorts her nature by reading forbidden books. All three push beyond traditional Judaism's narrow definition of female identity in perverted sexual relationships which mock the freedom they seek.

The intellectually conceived depravities of Shloimele and Lise seem graver than the instinctive debaucheries of Mendel, whose atheism is rooted in invincible ignorance. In his uninhibited life style Mendel is natural man but unnatural Jew, his thoughtless amorality generating the chaos unleashed by his more intelligent partners in corruption. For a Jew, no matter his intelligence, moral neutrality is impossible in Singer's dualistic world where God and Satan contend for human souls. Because God has long since given His chosen people the tools of salvation, they need only hew to the law and ignore Satan's blandishments. Satan, a skilled purveyor of sin, proves powerless against those whose faith remains unshaken even in the face of cataclysmic adversity. Despite his daughter Lise's suicide, Reb Bunim cannot be deflected from the path of righteousness. Perhaps as a reward for his unswerving faith that whatever God has ordained must go unquestioned, he escapes the apocalyptic fire and plague that devastate Kreshev soon after his departure. Reb Bunim's piety is not only valuable in its own right but is a means of resolving the dualities that underlie Singer's fiction. During his attempt to sway Reb Bunim, Satan digresses from his narration to explain that tempting people to transgress "is the purpose for which the Creator sent me down to earth" (129). Far from being God's coequal, Satan is merely his tool. Following the tradition of Jewish mysticism embodied in the cabala, Singer argues that "Satan makes creation possible" since without him "everything would be divinity, everything would be great and radiant . . . and there would be no place for individuality, for free choice."[7] God dims His radiance, employing Satan to force man to choose between good and evil. That the devastation of an entire town can result from the failure of three people to make the right choice—"And this was all because of a sin committed by a husband, a wife, and a coachman"—is the hard lesson of "The Destruction of Kreshev."

Allowed by God to range freely on earth, and privy to man's hidden desires, Satan has little trouble ferreting out likely targets and learning how to tempt them. The ideal omniscient narrator, he discovers his prospective victim's weakness, offers him the appropriate bait, traces his decline, and swoops down to claim his soul. Not only "Zeidlus the Pope" and "The Destruction of Kreshev," but "The Unseen" (1957), in which Nathan abandons his wife, Roise, to run away with the whorish servant, Shifra; and "The Mirror" (1955), in which Zirel is lead by vanity to accompany an imp to hell, are prominent among Singer's many stories involving triumphant Devil-narrators. A variation on this theme is played in "The Gentleman from Cracow" (1957) when Satan, rather than narrating the story, assumes the outwardly pleasing form of the title character.

THE SHORT STORIES

His sudden appearance in Frampol just after a drought, a hailstorm, and a plague of locusts had successively decimated an already dirt-poor *shtetl* is regarded by the desperate townspeople as "a gift from Heaven." The gold he squanders, apparently the salvation of Frampol, is, of course, Satan's ancient stock-in-trade. The ball he gives, ostensibly to gather together Frampol's eligible young women so that he may choose a bride, becomes the symbolic locus of the corruption he hopes to engender. Like similar balls in *The Family Moskat, The Manor,* and *The Estate,* this one is more appropriate for rich Gentiles than for pious Jews whose festivities are prescribed by law only for certain holidays. Attending such a ball is therefore tantamount to forsaking Jewishness—typified by the yeshiva students who abandon their holy books and by the young matrons who show up despite Rabbi Ozer's injunction. Already dazzled by the stranger's largesse, released from their inhibitions in the frenzied merrymaking of the ball, the Frampol Jews have laid themselves open to the disguised Devil's proposal that they draw lots for marriage partners. His offer of ten thousand ducats as dowry for each maiden who makes a mockery of the laws governing Jewish marriage sets up the moral choice that Singer's Jews must inevitably make. When they opt for the gentleman's gold

over Jewish law, thereby allying themselves with
Satan against God, their depravity is evidenced by
the grotesque couplings of boys with spinsters,
midgets with giants, and beauties with cripples
that result from the unholy marriage lottery. The
perversion that engenders these marriages finds
its ultimate expression in the union of the elegant
gentleman with Hodle, the town whore. Hodle's
"There is no God" renders explicit the blasphemy
implicit in the marriage lottery. As though unleashed by her words, a huge lightning bolt
"simultaneously struck the synagogue, the
study-house, and the ritual bath," those reposito-
ries of Jewishness which Frampol's transgressions
had already symbolically destroyed, setting the entire town on fire and revealing the gentleman as
Ketev Mriri, Chief of the Devils, and Hodle as
Lilith.

It is at this point, when Satan's reign is established in Frampol much as it was in Kreshev, that
"The Gentleman from Cracow" becomes more
than a cautionary moral tale. In the wake of the
conflagration that engulfs Kreshev, "a plague followed, men, women, and children perished, and
Kreshev was truly destroyed" (130). A perfunctory
notice that the town is later rebuilt does not ame-
liorate the lesson of "The Destruction of Kreshev":
the wages of sin are death. But in "The Gentleman

from Cracow" the apocalyptic flames which con-
sume innocent children, leaving only their charred
bones to be discovered by their anguished parents,
are also the harbingers of redemption. With all
their poverty the people of Frampol "had been
blessed with fine children," the ultimate Jewish
riches. By sacrificing their children on the altar of
their greed, they have exchanged the symbolic
wealth conferred by God for the spurious gold
proffered by the Devil. Whether contingent upon
the fact that their lust for gold has been forever
quelled—or upon the holiness of Rabbi Ozer, who
holds himself accountable for his peoples' sins and
whose house alone is spared the all-consum-
ing fire—their redemption turns "The Gentleman
from Cracow" into a parable of Jewish renewal. In
the new Frampol which rises from the ashes of the
old, "a gold coin became an abomination . . . and
even silver was looked at askance" (28). Succeed-
ing generations of inhabitants remain willing pau-
pers, welcoming poverty as the badge of
Jewishness. Welded together in a community of
the poor, the Frampol Jews revive the moral order
shattered by the anarchic rage for gold.

By doing communal penance for their sins the
Jews of Frampol enter a new and better world. A
product of their diligence, perseverance, unity,
and above all of their hard-won piety, the new or-

der could never have been achieved by the quick fix of the gentleman's gold. Only by hewing steadfastly to their ancient dispensation can Singer's Jews hope for salvation—in this world as well as the next. Taken together, "The Destruction of Kreshev" and "The Gentleman from Cracow" recapitulate the themes first announced by nearly identical means in *Satan in Goray*. From the outset of his career Singer distrusts the impulse to alter the world, which he habitually identifies with Satan's will toward chaos. Lust, pride, greed, ambition—all are variants of the false messianism which Singer first personifies in Sabbatai Zevi and which destroys individuals and communities alike. Jewish traditionalists who criticize Singer for his many unflattering portraits of, and apparent disloyalty to, his fellow Jews miss the point of his fiction. So relentlessly does Singer define transgression as deviation from Jewish law that his sinners become unwitting allies in preserving Jewish values. Only by doing penance and returning to those values can his sinners find the fulfillment they futilely sought elsewhere. The sexuality, criminality, and demonology which fill his pages and unnerve his orthodox critics are employed to celebrate the pious and humble life style they oppose. Honoring a people and a way of life that are no more but that are worthy of remembrance and emulation, Singer remains faithful to the values traditionally celebrated by Yiddish writers: "The virtue of powerlessness, the power of helplessness, the company of the dispossessed, the sanctity of the insulted and the injured—these, finally, are the great themes of Yiddish literature."[8]

Notes

1. Isaac Bashevis Singer, *Collected Stories* (New York: Farrar, Straus, 1982). Page references are to this edition unless otherwise noted.

2. Irving H. Buchen, *Isaac Bashevis Singer and the Eternal Past* (New York: New York University Press, 1968) 117.

3. Isaac Bashevis Singer and Richard Burgin, *Conversations with Isaac Bashevis Singer* (Garden City, NY: Doubleday, 1985) 101.

4. Singer and Burgin 101.

5. Paul N. Siegel, "Gimpel and the Archetype of the Wise Fool," *The Achievement of Isaac Bashevis Singer,* ed. Marcia Allentuck (Carbondale: Southern Illinois University Press, 1969) 162.

6. Morris Golden, "Dr. Fischelson's Miracle: Duality and Vision in Singer's Fiction," *The Achievement of Isaac Bashevis Singer* 40. The thirteenth-century *Zohar* is the earliest book of Jewish mystical writings which comprise the cabala.

7. Isaac Bashevis Singer and Irving Howe, "Yiddish Tradition vs. Jewish Tradition: A Dialogue," *Midstream* 19, (1973): 35.

8. Irving Howe and Eliezar Greenberg, eds., *A Treasury of Yiddish Stories* (New York: Viking, 1953) 38.

BIBLIOGRAPHY

Works by Isaac Bashevis Singer
Novels

The Family Moskat. Trans. A. H. Gross. New York: Noonday Press, 1950; London: Secker and Warburg, 1966. Published in Yiddish 1950. Serialized in Yiddish in the Jewish daily *Forward* 1945–1948.

Satan in Goray. Trans. Jacob Sloan. New York: Noonday Press, 1955; London: Owen, 1958. Published in Yiddish, Warsaw: 1935; New York: 1943, with five short stories.

The Magician of Lublin. Trans. Elaine Gottlieb and Joseph Singer. New York: Noonday Press, 1960; London: Secker and Warburg, 1961. Serialized in the *Forward* 1959.

The Slave. Trans. Isaac Bashevis Singer and Cecil Hemley. New York: Farrar, Straus, 1962; London: Secker and Warburg, 1963. Serialized in the *Forward* 1961.

The Manor. Trans. Joseph Singer and Elaine Gottlieb. New York: Farrar, Straus, 1967; London: Secker and Warburg, 1968. Serialized in the *Forward* 1953–1955.

The Estate. Trans. Joseph Singer, Elaine Gottlieb, and Elizabeth Shub. New York: Farrar, Straus, 1969; London: Cape, 1970. Serialized in the *Forward* 1953–1955.

Enemies, a Love Story. Trans. Aliza Shevrin and Elizabeth Shub. New York: Farrar, Straus, 1972; London: Cape, 1972. Serialized in the *Forward* 1966.

Shosha. Trans. Joseph Singer and Isaac Bashevis Singer. New York: Farrar, Straus, 1978; London: Cape, 1979. Serialized in the *Forward* 1974.

The Manor. Trans. Joseph Singer, Elaine Gottlieb, and Elizabeth Shub. New York: Farrar, Straus, 1979. One-volume edition of *The Manor* and *The Estate.*

The Penitent. New York: Farrar, Straus, 1983. Serialized in the *Forward,* 1974.

BIBLIOGRAPHY

Unpublished Novels

The Sinning Messiah. Serialized in the *Forward* 1935–1936.

Shadows on the Hudson. Serialized in the *Forward* 1957.

A Ship to America. Serialized in the *Forward* 1958.

Yarme and Kayle. Serialized in the *Forward* 1976.

Collections of Short Stories

Gimpel the Fool and Other Stories. New York: Noonday Press, 1957; London: Owen, 1958.

The Spinoza of Market Street. New York: Farrar, Straus, 1961; London: Secker and Warburg, 1962.

Short Friday and Other Stories. New York: Farrar, Straus, 1964; London: Secker and Warburg, 1967.

Selected Short Stories of Isaac Bashevis Singer. Ed. Irving Howe. New York: Modern Library, 1966.

The Séance and Other Stories. New York: Farrar, Straus, 1968; London: Cape, 1970.

A Friend of Kafka and Other Stories. New York: Farrar, Straus, 1970; London: Cape, 1972.

An Isaac Bashevis Singer Reader. New York: Farrar, Straus, 1971.

A Crown of Feathers and Other Stories. New York: Farrar, Straus, 1973; London: Cape, 1974.

Passions and Other Stories. New York: Farrar, Straus, 1975; London: Cape, 1976.

Old Love. New York: Farrar, Straus, 1979; London: Cape, 1980.

The Collected Stories. New York: Farrar, Straus, 1982; London: Cape, 1982.

The Image and Other Stories. New York: Farrar, Straus, 1985.

Memoirs

In My Father's Court. Trans. Channah Kleinerman-Goldstein, Elaine Gottlieb, and Joseph Singer. New York: Farrar,

BIBLIOGRAPHY

Straus, 1966; London: Secker and Warburg, 1967.

A Little Boy in Search of God; or, Mysticism in a Personal Light. With Ira Moskowitz. Garden City, NY: Doubleday, 1976.

A Young Man in Search of Love. Garden City, NY: Doubleday, 1978.

Lost in America. Garden City, NY: Doubleday, 1981.

Love and Exile. Garden City, NY: Doubleday, 1984. One-volume edition of the three preceding volumes, with a new introduction: "The Beginning."

Children's Books

Zlateh the Goat and Other Stories. Trans. Elizabeth Shub and the author. Illus. Maurice Sendak. New York: Harper and Row, 1966; Harmondsworth: Longman, Young, 1970.

The Fearsome Inn. Trans. Elizabeth Shub and the author. Illus. Nonny Hogrogian. New York: Scribner's, 1967; London: Collins, 1970.

Mazel and Shlimazel; or, The Milk of a Lioness. Trans. Elizabeth Shub and the author. Illus. Margot Zemach. New York: Farrar, Straus, 1967; London: Cape, 1979.

When Shlemiel Went to Warsaw and Other Stories. Trans. Channah Kleinerman-Goldstein, Elaine Gottlieb, and others. New York: Farrar, Straus, 1968; Harmondsworth: Longman, Young, 1974.

Elijah the Slave. Illus. Antonio Frasconi. New York: Farrar, Straus, 1970.

Joseph and Koza; or, The Sacrifice to the Vistula. Trans. Elizabeth Shub and the author. Illus. Symeon Shimin. New York: Farrar, Straus, 1970.

Alone in the Wild Forest. Trans. Elizabeth Shub and the author. Illus. Margot Zemach. New York: Farrar, Straus, 1971.

The Topsy-Turvy Emperor of China. Trans. Elizabeth Shub and the author. Illus. William Pene du Bois. New York: Harper and Row, 1971.

BIBLIOGRAPHY

The Wicked City. Trans. Elizabeth Shub and the author. Illus.
   Leonard Everett Fisher. New York: Farrar, Straus, 1972.
The Fools of Chelm and Their History. Trans. Elizabeth Shub
   and the author. Illus. Uri Shulevitz. New York: Farrar,
   Straus, 1973.
Why Noah Chose the Dove. Trans. Elizabeth Shub. Illus. Eric
   Carle. New York: Farrar, Straus, 1974.
A Tale of Three Wishes. Illus. Irene Lieblich. New York: Farrar,
   Straus, 1975.
Naftali the Storyteller and His Horse, Sus, and Other Stories.
   Trans. Joseph Singer, Ruth Schachner Finkel, and the
   author. Illus. Margot Zemach. New York: Farrar, Straus,
   1976; Oxford: Oxford University Press, 1977.
The Power of Light: Eight Stories for Hanukkah. New York:
   Farrar, Straus, 1980.
The Golem. New York: Farrar, Straus, 1982; London: Deutsch,
   1983.
Stories for Children. New York: Farrar, Straus, 1984.

Critical Works about Singer
Bibliography
Bryer, Jackson R., and Paul E. Rockwell. "Isaac Bashevis
   Singer in English: A Bibliography." *Critical Views of Isaac
   Bashevis Singer.* Ed. Irving Malin. New York: New York
   University Press, 1968. 220–65.
Books
Alexander, Edward. *Isaac Bashevis Singer.* Boston: Twayne,
   1980. This survey focuses on the novels, considering Singer
   as "a writer in the Jewish tradition but not exactly the
   Yiddish tradition."
Allentuck, Marcia, ed. *The Achievement of Isaac Bashevis Singer.*
   Carbondale: Southern Illinois University Press, 1969. This

BIBLIOGRAPHY

collection includes eleven essays printed for the first time, four dealing with recurring aspects of Singer's work, the remainder with single texts.

Buchen, Irving H. *Isaac Bashevis Singer and the Eternal Past.* New York: New York University Press; London: University of London Press, 1968. Singer records Jewish history through characters who symbolically embody aspects of that history. Eternal recurrence and timelessness are therefore crucial motifs in his fiction.

Kresh, Paul. *Isaac Bashevis Singer: The Magician of West 86th Street.* New York: Dial, 1979. This adulatory biography exhaustively surveys Singer's life and work to date.

Malin, Irving. *Isaac Bashevis Singer.* New York: Ungar, 1972. Malin prefers Singer's short stories and "closed novels"— those dealing with a single central consciousness—to the "open novels"—those dealing with many families and events.

_____, ed. *Critical Views of Isaac Bashevis Singer.* New York: New York University Press, 1969. This collection is divided equally between new essays and reprinted material and includes a comprehensive bibliography of works by and about Singer in English.

Miller, David Neal. *Fear of Fiction: Narrative Strategies in the Works of Isaac Bashevis Singer.* Albany: State University of New York Press, 1985. Concentrating on Singer's Yiddish stories and articles in the *Forward,* Miller argues that Singer undermines the reader's genre expectations by deliberately blurring the distinctions between fiction and reportage.

Sinclair, Clive. *The Brothers Singer.* London: Allison and Busby, 1983. In this comparative study of the Singer novels Sinclair traces the influence of Israel Joshua on his younger brother. Despite the outward resemblances of their family chronicles, however, "the final reference for Joshua was history, whereas for Bashevis it was religion."

Siegel, Ben. *Isaac Bashevis Singer.* Minneapolis: University of Minnesota Press, 1969. One of a series of pamphlets on American writers, this is a rapid-fire survey of Singer's work to date.

Articles and Parts of Books

Alexander, Edward. "The Destruction and Resurrection of the Jews in the Fiction of I. B. Singer." *The Resonance of Dust: Essays on Holocaust Literature and Jewish Fate.* 149–169. Columbus: Ohio State University Press, 1979. Singer's fictional treatment of the Holocaust is retrospective and/or symbolic rather than direct.

Baumgarten, Murray. *City Scriptures: Modern Jewish Writing.* Cambridge: Harvard University Press, 1982. 45–55. Abba's strong sense of self ("The Little Shoemakers") contrasts with Herman's fluidity (*Enemies*), enabling the former to reconstitute traditional Jewish life in America while the latter cannot.

Berger, Alan L. *Crisis and Covenant: The Holocaust in American Jewish Fiction.* Albany: State University of New York Press, 1985. 79–88. Because each of the major characters of *Enemies* represents an "aspect of Jewish existence after the catastrophe," the novel "reflects the theological turmoil of post-Holocaust Jewish existence."

Bilik, Dorothy Seidman. *Immigrant-Survivors: Post-Holocaust Consciousness in Recent Jewish American Fiction.* Middletown: Wesleyan University Press, 1981. 113–35. Herman's failure consists in evading the duty of memorializing the past and preserving the sense of community which motivates the more responsible characters in *Enemies*.

BIBLIOGRAPHY

Ellmann, Mary. "The Piety of Things in *The Manor.*" *The Achievement of Isaac Bashevis Singer.* Ed. Marcia Allentuck. Carbondale: Southern Illinois University Press, 1969. 124-44. Only by living piously can Jews cling to order and attain the good. Lacking piety they yield to irrational nature and shallow worldliness.

Fixler, Michael. "The Redeemers: Themes in the Fiction of Isaac Bashevis Singer." *Kenyon Review* 26 (1964): 371-86. Central to Singer's fiction is a vision of the redemptive destiny of the Jewish people.

Gittleman, Sol. *From Shtetl to Suburbia: The Family in Jewish Literary Imagination.* Boston: Beacon Press, 1978. 107-15. "The Little Shoemakers" is an idealized version of assimilation, "the perfect Jewish fairy tale for the Jew growing old in America."

Golden, Morris. "Dr. Fischelson's Miracle: Duality and Vision in Singer's Fiction." *The Achievement of Isaac Bashevis Singer.* Ed. Marcia Allentuck, Carbondale: Southern Illinois University Press, 1969. 27-43. Dr. Fischelson's union with Dobbe in "The Spinoza of Market Street," like the preserving deaths which conclude "Short Friday" and "A Wedding in Brownsville," ritualistically affirms faith in divine order.

Hochman, Baruch. "I. B. Singer's Vision of Good and Evil." *Midstream* 13 (1969): 66-73. Of the novels to date, all but *The Family Moskat* "are parables of conversion, in which the primary relationship is between man and God, not between man and man."

Howe, Irving. Introduction. *Selected Short Stories of Isaac Bashevis Singer.* New York: Modern Library, 1966. The literary modernism that contributes so much to Singer's popularity in translation disturbs readers weaned on the Yiddish traditions of sentimentality and social concern.

BIBLIOGRAPHY

Madison, Charles. "I. Bashevis Singer—Novelist of Hasidic Gothicism." *Yiddish Literature: Its Scope and Major Writers.* New York: Ungar, 1968. 479-99. Singer writes about what he knows best—"the Hasidic aspects of Jewish life."

Mucke, Edith. "Isaac B. Singer and Hassidic Philosophy." *Minnesota Review* 7 (1967): 214-21. Singer's fiction is imbued with the Hasidic spirit of his father's rabbinical court. No justice exists in the absence of godliness.

Pinsker, Sanford. "The Fictive Worlds of I. B. Singer." *Critique* 11 (1969): 26-39. Singer holds in delicate balance the real and imaginative worlds. "Gimpel the Fool" and *The Magician of Lublin* embody the conscious retreat from external reality into the internal world of the imagination.

Siegel, Ben. "Sacred and Profane: Isaac Bashevis Singer's Embattled Spirits." *Critique* 6 (1963): 24-47. Forces of good and evil war for the souls of Singer's protagonists. Crucial to his fiction are those moments of revelation which expose their common humanity.

Siegel, Paul. "Gimpel and the Archetype of the Wise Fool." *The Achievement of Isaac Bashevis Singer.* Ed. Marcia Allentuck, Carbondale: Southern Illinois University Press, 1969. 159-73. Siegel argues that the wise or sainted fool represented by Gimpel is "not merely a recurring character in Yiddish fiction; he is a centuries-old archetypal figure of Western literature."

Zatlin, Linda G. "The Themes of Isaac Bashevis Singer's Short Fiction." *Critique* 11 (1969): 40-46. No matter the time or locale of Singer's stories, they invariably focus on the modern problem of finding a viable faith. For Singer this involves choosing God instead of Satan.

Interviews

Blocker, Joel, and Richard Elman. "An Interview with Isaac Bashevis Singer." *Commentary* Nov. 1963: 364-72.

BIBLIOGRAPHY

Pondrom, Cyrena N. "Isaac Bashevis Singer: An Interview and a Biographical Sketch." *Contemporary Literature* 10 (1969): 1–38; 332–51.

Singer, Isaac Bashevis, and Richard Burgin. *Conversations with Isaac Bashevis Singer.* Garden City, NY: Doubleday, 1985.

Singer, Isaac Bashevis, and Irving Howe. "Yiddish Tradition vs. Jewish Tradition: A Dialogue." *Midstream* 19, (1973): 33–38.

INDEX

INDEX

INDEX

INDEX

INDEX